Daylighting
Natural Light in Architecture

(2017)

Other books in this series

Lighting Historic Buildings, McGraw-Hill, 1997   ISBN 0070498644
Lighting Modern Buildings, Architectural Press, 2000   ISBN 0750640820
The Lit Environment, Architectural Press, 2002   ISBN 0750648899
Daylighting: Natural Light in Architecture, Architectural Press, 2004   ISBN 0750663235

Daylighting

Natural Light in Architecture

Derek Phillips

With a foreword by

Carl Gardner

AMSTERDAM • BOSTON • HEIDELBERG • LONDON • NEW YORK • OXFORD
PARIS • SAN DIEGO • SAN FRANCISCO • SINGAPORE • SYDNEY • TOKYO

Architectural Press is an imprint of Elsevier

ELSEVIER

Architectural
Press

Architectural Press
An imprint of Elsevier
Linacre House, Jordan Hill, Oxford OX2 8DP
200 Wheeler Road, Burlington, MA 01803

First published 2004

British Library Cataloguing in Publication Data
Phillips, Derek, 1923-
    Daylighting: natural light in architecture
    1. Daylighting   2. Lighting, Architectural and decorative
    I. Title
    729.2'8

ISBN 0 7506 6323 5

Library of Congress Cataloguing in Publication Data
A catalogue record for this book is available from the Library of Congress

For information about all Architectural Press publications
visit our website at http://books.elsevier.com/architecturalpress

Typeset by Keyword Typesetting Services Ltd, Wallington, Surrey
Printed and bound in Italy

Contents

Architect: Foster and Partners
Lighting Design: Claude Engle
Client: Federal Republic of Germany

Dedication

To DIANA HESKETH, Sculptor

"The life that I have, is all that I have
  and the life that I have is yours.

The love that I have, of the life that I have,
  is yours and yours and yours"[1]

---

[1] The quotation is taken from the poem written for Violette Czabo as a code, when, as a member of SOE, she was an agent in Churchill's secret army. She was later shot by the Germans as a spy. Marks, Leo C. (1998) *Between Silk and Cyanide*, Free Press.

Acknowledgements

It would be tedious to name all the architects who were kind enough to provide information for the case studies in this book, in terms of the diagrams and images of their work; for this it will be sufficient to refer to the case studies where they are shown, for which I am most grateful.

As to others I would like to express my gratitude to four lighting consultant practices who have provided information of their daylighting design work. These are Max Fordham, Buro Happold, DPA Lighting Consultants, and Hoare Lee; all these offices were most generous with their time and assistance.

As to others, I would particularly thank David Loe for his advice and guidance, together with the many other people who have been unstinting in providing information. The faults you may find in this book are all mine. I should perhaps add that this book is the last in the series of books I have written on the subject of lighting for Architectural Press, and in saying this, to thank their staff for producing what I hope will be seen as both a well designed and useful series.

Foreword

By Carl Gardner M. Sc. (Arch) FILE
Editor of *The Lighting Journal*

In the annals of twentieth century architecture daylight and sunlight have had rather uneasy fortunes. Prior to the development of electric light on a commercial scale at the end of the nineteenth century, daylight had, of course, been absolutely essential to indoor work, leisure and habitation for almost as long as human beings had been building homes. Even the invention of oil lamps, candles, torches and gas lighting, important as they were, could not seriously displace daylight and sunlight for the purpose of interior lighting.

The result was a rich, extensive history of innovations of building design to bring more and more natural light into the interior: one thinks of the clerestorey window, glazed cupola and glazed curtain wall in ecclesiastical architecture – and roof lights, bow windows and the full-height sash windows in residential buildings.

Even in the early twentieth century daylight innovations continued with features such as the fully glazed facade and the large-scale atrium.

However, somewhere in the middle of the twentieth century natural lighting started to be seen as a problem – something to be excluded, or at least curtailed, particularly in the commercial building sector.

Post-war 'technicist' notions of management suggested that sophisticated electrical lighting and air-conditioning systems were far superior ways of managing the interior office environment, compared with all that wild, uncontrollable daylight, sunlight and fresh air.

So we saw a generation of buildings with restricted, poorly designed (and invariably non-opening) fenestration, deep floor plates, intensive air-conditioning and mind-numbingly repetitive grids of recessed fluorescent lighting. The result we now realize, was most probably a huge reduction in working efficiency, an epidemic of eye-strain, headaches and personal malaise – and an incalculable loss of working hours through sickness and absenteeism.

The aggregate of all these effects was summed up in the 1980s by the phrase 'sick building syndrome'. Things had to change.

So, over the last 15 or 20 years, we have begun to witness a substantial rethink. This reassessment of the role and contribution of natural resources such as fresh air and daylight has had two main thrusts. First, there has been the recognition that access to daylight and outside views are important psychological factors in human well-being which vastly over-ride any incidental problems that unpredictable sunlight can throw up.

Second, driven by the threat of 'global warming' there has been the constant push to reduce energy use in buildings – and what better way to do so than to make use of the free, environmentally friendly energy provided by the sun, in the form of daylight, in all its rich and wondrous intensity.

The undeniable truth is that the optimum, and effective use, of daylight in buildings is both good for people and the environment. Already in the form of some marvellously innovative building designs (some of which are showcased in these pages) we have started to see the results of this new-found recognition. However, helped by a plethora of new building materials and technologies, we are hopefully only at the beginning of a whole new stage in architectural daylight design, which could surpass everything that has gone before.

So this is a most appropriate time to publish a study of this kind, which both refreshes our knowledge of the past and looks to the future. Let us hope that its publication and dissemination will help stimulate this important and ongoing debate about the use of natural lighting in twenty-first century architecture.

Carl Gardner

Preface

Whilst my earlier books have been directed mainly at architects, who I felt most needed some advice on artificial sources of light, and the environments which can be created by good design. This was based on the assumption that architects had an innate sense of the role played by daylighting developed over a thousand years in which there was no viable alternative.

The present book is directed not so much towards architects as towards the lighting profession, by which I mean the industry who provide the technical means and equipment, and the designers who work their magic in the creation of beautifully lit interiors.

Daylighting has always been the poor relation of the industry ... there was no money in it ... and whilst paying lip service to the concept of daylighting it has been left to the scientists to come up with new ideas, none of which tell an architect much more than was known in the days of Byzantium.

I have asked some of the major players in the industry, both manufacturers and designers, whether they offer daylight advice to architects and the answer has, apart from one or two shining exceptions, been an embarrassed 'no'.

The purpose of this book, at a time of renewed interest in 'sustainability', is to make a rational argument for considering daylight first, what are the arguments in favour of a daylight approach, and then to show by means of a series of case studies how architects, often in conflict with engineering advice, have created buildings in which natural light has been shown to play a major strategic role in the development of the design of the building.

Introduction

HISTORY

The history of daylighting dates of course from the beginning of time, starting with natural light entering the mouths of caves. After 1900 daylight was in competition with the various forms of artificial light, up to the point when it appeared to be irrelevant, having as its nadir the development of 'Burolandschaft', when buildings lit by artificial light sources could be of infinite depth, and when even some schools and factories were built without any windows at all.

There are many reasons for the renewed interest in daylighting, the increasing cost of fossil fuels and the realization that sources of electricity have a finite life, being quoted as most cogent; but perhaps even more important are the less tangible aspects of daylighting which relate more to the human spirit and the need for a quality of life.

ENVIRONMENT

What are these less tangible aspects? None of them on their own might be thought to be of primary importance; it is when they are added together and a holistic view taken of the interior environment which they create that their importance becomes paramount.

Taken in no order of priority they can be listed as the following:

1. Change and variety
   The human desire for change wrought by the changes in the seasons, the weather and the time of day.

2. Modelling
   The direction of natural light providing the shadow patterns which inform the appearance of objects and surfaces, and give them the appearance that we associate with the natural world.

3. Orientation
   Orientation is of importance not only in the external siting of buildings to maximize the influence of diurnal change, but to enable those within a building to establish themselves in relation to the world outside.

4. Sunlight effect
   When it is available sunlight has a therapeutic effect and the importance of access to a degree of sunlight during the day is most noticeable when it is denied.

5. Colour
   Natural colour may vary throughout the day, but it is the standard by which all colour is judged, and there is no artificial source which can match it.

6. View out
   Access to a view out may not have been paramount in the minds of the early building designers, but it is not only in the twentieth century that the view from buildings has been conceived to be of some importance.

A discussion of the various intangibles leads to the consideration of aspects of health and daylighting, from Seasonal Affective Disorder or SAD, to the beneficial effect of sunlight.

WINDOWS

The design of windows is in constant development, both in the form of the aperture through which the daylight comes and in the nature of glass or transparent material permitting the light to enter.

Forgetting about the early architecture, such as the Pantheon or the Roman patio house, where holes were left in the roof admitting rain as well as light, it was left to the eighteenth century and the introduction of the glazed rooflight, to introduce daylight into the interior of a building. This development had the important effect of increasing the 'daylight effective depth' and has its modern equivalent in the atriums we see today, the word atrium being devised from the original Roman patio house.

There are many window forms which have been developed over the centuries, some for military reasons, and others designed to introduce light into the interior in such a manner as to reduce the difference in brightness between the inside and outside to reduce glare, to the point where the wall became the window and some form of control is required to protect the occupant from excessive brightness.

The control of sunlight is sometimes necessary, more so in parts of the world other than in the western hemisphere, and many ingenious devices have been designed to cope with this, some of which are at odds with the less tangible benefits of daylighting enumerated above and pay attention more to architectural fashion than functional design.

The importance of the introduction of daylight to modern building interiors can be measured by the innovative methods often employed. These include the use of 'light pipes' where glazed holes are left in the roof and daylight is then directed to lower parts of the building through ducts, or by means of heliostats placed on the roof which track the sun.

ENERGY

The energy used by artificial lighting in buildings is a major part of the energy use in buildings and it is recognized that if this can be reduced and consequently the emissions of carbon dioxide[1] this will assist in the reduction of greenhouse gases and have an important effect in reducing global warming. The greater use of daylight will lead to a reduction in the use of electrical energy and assist significantly in the battle to solve the energy crisis.

Whilst there are climates in the world where the use of methods of air-conditioning are considered to be mandatory, there is some ambivalence among building owners as to whether the climate in this country demands its use. A passive response building in which the maximum use is made of natural light and ventilation, can be both comfortable and cost effective, whilst making undoubted savings in the use of running costs and energy.

It is not suggested that daylight can in all circumstances replace artificial light entirely during the day, but by the use of 'daylight linking controls' the use of electrical energy can be significantly reduced.

One should not over-simplify, since there are some areas in buildings where daylight can never reach and electric light will always be required; just as there are some buildings, such as homes, where electric light will rarely be necessary during daylight hours. A careful study of the plans related to energy efficient daylighting design will indicate where sufficient daylight is available, and where it will need to be supplemented.

The new science of photovoltaics where the glass skin of the building is used for solar collection is in its infancy; but the possibilities for energy savings are obvious, and this is where architects have a role to play, as important as the established needs for the introduction of alternative sources of energy from wave or wind.

HUMAN FACTORS

Daylight is inextricably linked with windows, and windows let in more than light; they have associations with the admission of heat and of heat loss, solar gain and with the admission of noise; they are closely related to air movement and the need for ventilation.

It is impossible to judge the need for daylight and sunlight in engineering terms alone, the human factor is at least of equal importance. People like daylight, and in some countries such as the Netherlands and Germany, there are regulations determining that in a work situation, the staff must not be located further than six metres from a window. Daylight is essential in providing a pleasant visual environment, contributing to a feeling of wellbeing.

During daylight hours in a work situation where people are in a fixed position most of the time, the method of lighting is clearly crucial and those situations where people work in entirely artificial conditions are liable to lead to ill health and absenteeism.

Some of the most successful installations are where the control system leads to a system of 'daylight linking,' where daylight penetration is combined with artificial sources, in such a way that the space appears to be daylit during the day, but where some areas are supplemented by

---

[1]*New Light on Windows*. RIBA Seminar Nov. 1996
'Carbon dioxide emissions alone could be reduced by 94 million tonnes per year', Prof. Peter F. Smith.

artificial light for some or all of the day. It is the appearance of being daylight coupled with a relationship to the view outside the window which is of importance.

Apart from the provision of daylight, windows may be associated with the need for air movement and draught-free ventilation, whilst at the same time coping with the problems of noise and dirt pollution. Together with the engineering solutions to the problems of heat loss in winter and heat gain in summer, the window is at the leading edge of a solution to the human needs it must satisfy.

DAYLIGHT CALCULATION

The first and most obvious thing to understand is that daylight is variable: it varies with the seasons of the year, the time of day, and the weather.

For this reason the means of calculation are based on relative rather than absolute values, and this is usually defined in terms of the relationship between the light available outside, and that available at different positions inside, a proportion known as the daylight factor. By calculating the DF at a number of points throughout a space, an average DF can be assessed.

The simplest situations are those where the windows are placed in the vertical elevations of a building, and simple calculation methods are available to work out the daylight factors in the rooms adjacent to the windows. Where it is usually agreed that for average conditions, as represented by an overcast sky in the British climate, then the daylight inside will be a given percentage of the daylight available outside. The following values are correct if the unobstructed overcast sky provides an illuminance of 5000 lux.

For example a 1 per cent DF will give a light level of 50 lux, a 2 per cent DF will give a light level of 100 lux. The latter being a figure considered to be sufficient to provide a sense of the room being daylit, but not sufficient to carry out normal office tasks.

A 2 per cent DF would therefore be a space requiring artificial light for a large part of the year, whilst 5% would provide a 'well daylit space' for a large part of the day. Due to the variable nature of daylight a diffuse sky can produce 5000 lux or more for 85 per cent of the day, or lower for the remaining 15 per cent.

Lighting design offices will no doubt have the necessary computer software to calculate the amount of daylight in rooms lit by side windows; but where an architectural programme demands complicated building sections, there are computational methods available to assess the likely daylight penetration; these will generally demand the use of computers, and at the end of the day the cost involved can be heavy, and the outcome uncertain, bearing in mind the variable nature of the source.

The use of simple architectural models is useful here, since they are relatively simple to construct, can be altered easily to permit experimentation with change, and measurements taken of the inside and outside illuminance levels to provide daylight factors. These measurements may be made in daylight conditions outside, or in special cases such as art galleries, where illuminance levels are critical, by the use of an artificial sky designed to represent the exterior condition at any time of the year in different weather conditions. But perhaps the greatest advantage to the architect will be in the visual appearance of the interior spaces under different conditions, something which the architect can understand more readily than a series of numbers.

There are two main design considerations concerned with the orientation of the building. First there are new buildings placed on a greenfield site, where the architect has control of the orientation of its location, and where the needs of daylighting can inform the initial building strategy; then there are those buildings on restricted sites where the neighbouring buildings must be considered as obstructions, affecting the amount of daylight penetration, and likewise that your building does not obstruct your neighbour.

Where there are adjacent buildings these may enjoy certain rights of light, and these must be taken into account; in much the same way that the architect's own building, when complete, will have its own 'right to light'. It is important therefore for the architect to ensure that the profile of the building to be constructed complies in all respects with the planning laws, and observes the right of his neighbours' light. This can be something of a minefield, and specialist consultants are available to assist.

CASE STUDIES

Finally some examples of buildings are identified and studied to show how the needs of daylighting have informed the architect's design strategy, and how this is translated into the built form. The case studies are designed to show how daylight may have a greater or lesser effect in different architectural programmes, and will identify where one or more of the intangible factors will have had a disproportionate influence on the design. The aim is to illustrate that there are virtually no buildings where daylighting will not have a part to play.

Part 1

1 History

Windows ... architectural development ... takeover of artificial lighting ... renewal of interest in daylight ... energy use ... passive architecture ... strategy ... control

'It is impossible to overestimate the important influence of natural light on the interior and exterior forms of buildings and on those who dwell in them. So daylight is the natural beginning'[1].

From the earliest caves, daylight informed the lives of the inhabitants, initially in the difference between night and day; but as dwellings became more sophisticated, by means of openings or windows letting in light.

The history of architecture is synonymous with the history of the window and of daylighting from the initial crude openings, letting in light and air, heat and cold, the window was the vehicle for the introduction of daylight, and ultimately to the wondrous interiors of the mediaeval cathedral, the Baroque churches or the many private buildings of the eighteenth century.

The window has developed over the centuries, but its purpose of letting in daylight has remained its primary role; window openings required a suitable infill to modify the external climate. At first various materials were used, such as thin slabs of marble, sheets of mica or oiled paper, but it was not until the development of glass for windows that substantial progress could really be made.

Glass had been discovered as early as 3000 BC in Egypt, and was used for decorative objects, but it is known that small panes of hand-blown glass set into bronze frames were used for the infill to window openings during the Roman period. These were little different to the leaded lights of the mediaeval period, being limited to the small pane sizes governed by the manufacturing process.

It was left until the seventeenth century for large panes of glass to be developed in England and for larger windows to be made possible.

The history of windows is really the history of architecture, from the crude openings in the sides of early domestic buildings open to the atmosphere, or openings in the roof construction, allowing the entry of rain collected in a central pool.

---

[1]*Lighting Historic Buildings*. Architectural Press. 1997

The appearance of buildings of all periods reflects the nature of the windows, in some cases such as the mediaeval period, the shape and location of the windows being functionally related to the role played by daylighting, whilst in the renaissance period the location and form of windows became more formalized, often being less well related to the interior spaces they served ... the elevation, the appearance of the building seen from the outside, became of prime importance, a consideration which lingers on today.

Windows have always led to innovation, and this can be seen in the stained glass windows of the great mediaeval cathedrals, telling the Christian story, where whole walls of glass were made possible by structures such as the flying buttress.

Windows had to serve military needs in fortifed buildings, leading to slit windows from which arrows could be fired; with splayed sides having the desirable effect of reducing the contrast between the brightness of the window and the interior wall surface, a device which has continuing validity.

A further innovative means of daylighting was that developed for the lighting of the Baroque churches of southern Germany, where 'indirect' daylight onto the ornate decorations and ornaments of the church is gained from windows concealed from the direct view of the congregation. Indirect daylighting is equally valid today, as used by Basil Spence at Coventry Cathedral, or by Jorn Utson at the Bagsvaerd Church in Denmark[2].

Whilst the vertical windows set into the outside walls of buildings were clearly of the first importance, and continue to be so today, it was the roof lights allowing daylight into the central parts of buildings that had an important influence on the plan form of the stately homes of the seventeenth and eighteenth centuries. These took several forms, from domes such as that at Keddleston Hall (1759) where light enters from the top or Chiswick House (1725) where the dome is surrounded by windows in the sides, in both cases the method of daylighting allowed architects to have more flexibility to plan the central areas of their buildings. It is of interest that this method of introducing daylight to the centre of buildings has a resonance with the atria which we see in many buildings today.

The modern movement in England in the 1930s used the new methods of construction available, to allow an entirely new approach in residential buildings, with whole walls of glass and wrap-around windows at corners to express the freedom of the relationship between inside and outside, a freedom which was ultimately expressed in the walls of glass now possible in tall commercial structures.

Daylighting remained the primary means of lighting to all types of building until the early twentieth century, when for various reasons, not least the greater efficiency in the development of electric sources, the primary role of daylighting was beginning to be questioned.

The growth of the workplace in the nineteenth century had seen buildings requiring higher levels of light, and this was achieved by planning long horizontal windows, where the daylight close to the window wall would have been sufficient, but with the pressure to reduce the floor to floor height for economies of structure, even this became insufficient.

---

[2]*Lighting Modern Buildings*. Architectural Press.

The pressure to increase the levels of light in buildings came from the utility companies, who saw this as a means of increasing the sale of electricity, and for the manufacturers the sale of lamps and equipment. Up to a point this was a benign influence, although the effect in the USA went too far, with levels of 1000 Lux and above recommended where far less was sufficient.

By the 1960s the concept had grown that ultimately, if not immediately, artificial or electric lighting would supplant natural light as the primary source during the day in the work situation.

Quoting from the author's own book written in 1964:

> 'It is inevitable that artificial light must become the primary light source where efficiency of vision is combined with an economic analysis of building function. Natural lighting is becoming a luxury.'[3].

The fact that this was not deemed stupid at the time is a measure of how far down the road of the controlled environment life had become.

There was in fact substantial evidence to support this view for the lighting in offices, factories and other buildings where difficult visual tasks need to be done. Economies of structure had meant that ceiling heights had been lowered, reducing the penetration of daylight into buildings. A government 'low cost energy policy' determined that the price of electricity was not a major factor in the running costs of such buildings, and that therefore an economic case could be made.

By the 1960s a professor of architecture stated that the first decision an architect had to make when planning a new building was the level of light and the nature of the electric light source to achieve this.[4] ... daylight was to be disregarded as a functional source. This led to windowless factories, and even windowless schools, the ultimate idiocy. It was even mooted that buildings could be heated by the means of lighting, leading to artificial lighting being used at all times of day, even when the heat generated had to be wasted, by dispersal.

This was an 'engineering-led approach' and some architects tended to be carried along with it, although it must be said that the more thoughtful architects resisted.

It was not until the energy crisis, and the realization that our reliance on fossil fuels had limitations, that people started to question this high energy approach, and began to look at ways to reduce the electricity load in buildings, and one of the more obvious ways was to return to an understanding of the natural resource of daylight.

Clearly daylight is not cost free, and factors such as the control of sunlight, heat gain and loss, the association of windows with ventilation and the question of whether the windows should open or the building be sealed, are all problems which need to be addressed; but these need to be equated with the human desire for association with the natural environment, as well as the possible savings in electricity and cost.

It is useful to state some of the reasons why the association with the natural environment has been important, seen through the hindsight of history.

1. First there is the question of light for seeing in order to function within a space. This must vary according to the type of building, whether

---

[3]*Lighting in Architectural Design*. McGraw-Hill. 1964. Pub.USA
[4]Prof. Alex Hardy.

a residence, an office or a factory ... the need may be to read a book, operate a piece of machinery, or whatever. If it is possible for daylight to provide this, then we expect it to do so.

2. The natural appearance of a space, where the overall experience, the objects and surfaces, are modelled in daylight together with the addition of sunlight at certain times of day.

3. The cyclical change from morning to evening, changes which are varied still further with the weather and the season of the year. Man has an innate desire for variety and change in his environment, and changes in the appearance of a space from time to time provide this.

4. The orientation which comes with the knowledge of a person's whereabouts in relation to the outside world. In a totally artificial environment, a person has difficulty in finding his way inside a building, a problem which was evident in some of the early artificially lit shopping centres, where people became disoriented, having problems in finding their way around the building.

5. The experience of the world beyond the building, by the view to the outside, whilst this is associated with the factor of orientation, it has the added aspect of content ... which can be of open countryside, trees and landscape, but more often than not of other buildings and street patterns. What is important is not only the content but also the experience of something at a distance as a rest centre for the eye. Daylight is clearly crucial.

6. The experience of natural colour; for whilst the physical colour of our world as experienced in daylight changes from morning to night, the changes are a part of our experience; we compensate automatically, a white wall appears a white wall even if in the evening it may be warmer, or is coloured by sunlight, or altered by cloud formations ... it is the colour we regard as natural.

7. Although perhaps not essential, it is a part of the experience of the natural world that we should be able to receive natural ventilation, by opening windows. This is a part of the human desire for control of his environment, whether this be the light on his work, or the air that he breathes.

On the whole architects had not submitted easily to the tendency towards the totally artificial environment leading inevitably toward air-conditioning in larger projects; but tended to be overruled by engineers; however research work carried out in Britain by Prof. Hopkinson at the Building Research Station in the 1950s developed the concept of PSALI or Permanent Supplementary Artificial Lighting for Interiors[5].

The concept behind this research was that provided daylight at the side of the room closest to the window was adequate, the fall-off of light furthest from the window could be supplemented by electric sources.

This provided for the historic advantages of daylight listed earlier, most particularly in providing the impression that the whole room was daylit, although it was not, permitting the concept of the 'well lit room'. Whilst this did not have the immediate effect of reinstating daylight as a primary source it was left to other outside influences to reinforce the architect's renewed interest in the subject.

The outside influences were to some extent political, the sharp increase in oil prices and the fuel crisis, the gradual realization that the fossil fuels

---

[5]Paper by Ralph Hopkinson and James Longmore. PSALI. 1959

upon which the world relied, the coal and oil, had a finite life and once used were not replaceable. No doubt this would have been ignored apart from the further factor of a greater understanding of the greenhouse effect due to the release of carbon dioxide by the burning of those same fossil fuels. Finally there was the destruction of the ozone layer and the increasing danger of global warming.

For these reasons some nations took account of the need for an intense look at alternative means of energy, by means of wind and wave, and the use of hydroelectric power where this was possible.

This was all taking place at a time when the amount of energy in buildings was increasing, by means of the greater introduction of air-conditioning to a point when it was apparent that buildings had become the greatest single form of atmospheric pollution. Whilst this was clearly the prime mover in calling a pause to the rise in the use of energy in buildings, the role of the historic advantages of daylight were not insignificant, the human factors demanding a closer look.

The historic result of this was that buildings, analysed as the greatest cause of the problem, came under intense scrutiny; the words 'passive building' and 'sustainable architecture' became of greater importance. People began to seek ways to reduce the use of energy in buildings, and the prime suspect became the energy used for lighting.

Passive architecture, is where the structure of the building is designed in such a manner as to reduce the need for mechanical controls of heat, light and sound to a minimum: the term 'Net Zero Energy Demand' or a situation where 'the energy consumed equals the energy harvested.'

Daylight and sunlight are at the heart of this new philosophy; they arrive every day in greater or lesser quantity, and provide power for lighting in two ways. First they enter the building through openings as 'light' to the interior spaces and second they impact with the exterior building surfaces, and can be translated into energy by means of solar conversion.

What it does mean is that daylight must be at the centre of the architect's strategy by the orientation of the building, by the nature of the apertures, indeed the whole structure of the building.

This brings us back to the question of the infill of the apertures, at the building's perimeter ... this is no longer glass just to keep out the weather, but a very sophisticated window element which may be designed to restrict or harvest the exterior energy, by means of selected coatings, photovoltaics, cavity fills and advanced blind systems and controls. It is in such ways that the amount of energy used for lighting can be substantially reduced, contributing towards the ideal suggested of 'net zero energy demand'.

It is clear that daylighting is at the heart of the equation, requiring a holistic approach to design, in which the human factors outlined above can now be placed in the correct order of priority; it is no longer true (if it ever was) that daylight is a luxury concerned with the view out of the window, although the view out of the window is an essential part of the role that daylight must play.

In David Lloyd Jones's thoughtful book *Architecture and the Environment*, he defines sustainability in architecture as

> 'development that meets the needs of the present, and is at least as valuable to future generations as the value of the environmental exploitation that results ... a sustainable building (in energy terms) is one that over its life breaks even or is in credit in respect of energy consumption.'

If daylight is to be at the heart of this equation, then the use of energy for artificial lighting in buildings must be reduced by the intelligent use of daylighting design; since it is now possible for the deficit in energy to be made up by means of solar conversion ... the use of photovoltaics, powerful enough to generate sufficient energy to meet or exceed its lifetime consumption.

Sustainable architecture is associated with minimizing all the different aspects of energy consumption associated with the production of a building from materials to construction methods and transportation, together with the continuing operation of the building throughout its life; but it is with the energy used for artificial lighting and the possible economies associated with sunlight and daylight that we are concerned with here ... the development of a strategy for design, a strategy which involves all the relevant criteria leading towards a holistic solution.

If we ignore the demands made upon a 'passive' structure, by aspects of ventilation, air pollution, and the artificial lighting system, it is possible to outline a simple four-point strategy for daylighting design, bearing in mind that all the other factors need to be borne in mind to complete a holistic approach towards the building design.

1. A decision needs to be made on the siting of the building, differing as to its location and site characteristics; in a green field or urban situation; taking into account the orientation, sun path and location of existing buildings or landscape.

2. The building function may determine the room dimensions, heights, and subdivisions, bearing in mind the present and future needs of occupation. Room height is a key decision, having a bearing on daylight penetration and the desirable overall room depth as well as building costs.

3. The window size and disposition. This is clearly the most complicated design decision, since it must incorporate all the human factors mentioned earlier, such as the provision of view, control of heat gain and loss and the elimination of glare, as well as the more obvious needs of functional vision.

The combined windows should provide an average 5 per cent daylight factor for a substantial part of the floor space. From the architect's viewpoint, this may well appear as the most important decision, since it will determine the appearance of the building elevations from the exterior; but from a strategic point of view it will determine the success of the daylighting approach.

It will be advisable to prepare a specification for the windows to include the nature of the glass, its transmission value and other characteristics. The types of glass are discussed in some detail under the subject of energy later, but it is at this point that the needs of other disciplines must be integrated, such as ventilation, sound attenuation and energy conversion (PVs).

4. Finally control systems are a consideration, first, those controls which relate to the outside condition, the control of sunlight and the avoidance of glare; and second, those of the interior, the relationship with daylight and the artificial lighting system, to facilitate 'daylight linking'; this will be crucial to effect the possible savings in energy.

Whilst the four-fold decisions outlined are a necessary start, they must at each point be related to the other criteria for building design, not least of which will be the question of structural possibility, durability and its relationship to overall building costs, both initial and running costs, which relate to overall sustainability.

2 Environment

Change and variety ... modelling ... orientation ... sunlight ... colour ... view ... health

Various aspects of the environment which affect the interior appearance of buildings have been identified in the introductory chapter, and it is the purpose here to illustrate these aspects in more detail.

CHANGE/VARIETY

Perhaps the most obvious and certainly the most important aspect of daylighting is its capacity for change, leading to the infinite variety in appearance of the daylit interior. Change is at the heart of daylighting, the human body has a capacity for adaptation, particularly in vision, and the need to exercise this response.

Perception reacts to a degree of change; it is the natural order of things that the appearance of interior spaces alter with time; and if we have confidence in their continuing reality, it is because change in their lit appearance allows us to continue an exploration of the spaces we inhabit; an entirely different measure of experience to the static qualities of spaces lit entirely by artificial sources of light during the day; or where there is no access to the daylight outside. There is a natural process of renewal in the photochemical processes of the eye as it adapts to accommodate changes in daylight

First there is the natural change from day to night, from first light until dark and the need for artificial sources to take over when daylight fades. Then there are the changes associated with changes of the weather; from bright sunny days to dark and cloudy or rainy days, there is little doubt that the human spirit soars when rising in the morning on a bright day, an experience which is less likely to happen when it is dark and gloomy outside.

Closely associated with changes in the weather are those of the changes of season, from the winter snows to summer sunlight; each season will have its own character, which as human beings we accommodate to in our own way; but what is important is that the world outside, as experienced through the window, provides necessary information of the variety of the exterior world; whilst leading to subtle changes in the appearance of the interior.

Statue at the Tate Modern in the Turbine Hall, daylit

MODELLING

Modelling of a shape derives from its physical form, whether round, square or otherwise, coupled with the way in which light plays on its surfaces. This is referred to as its modelling and when this derives from daylight or sunlight, giving light from a single direction, this provides a form which is perceived by the eye as having meaning, unambiguous. This is a different experience again from the form of an object or space resulting from a room lit by artificial light, where the overall light may be received from a multitude of light sources.

The most usual daylight modelling is that derived from vertical windows at the side of a room, giving light from a single direction; this may be helped by windows from an adjacent wall which adds to the modelling; as the light will still be from the same overall direction, but adding to the total modelling.

Two examples might be used to emphasize this, the first, a Greek Doric column where the light of day gives modelling to the entasis on the rounded surfaces of the column; light which emphasizes its particular rounded quality together with its verticality. The second example is the original David statue by Michelangelo seen in its setting in the art gallery in Florence, lit from daylight above, where the form changes in time as the day goes by.

A more modern example of the use of overhead daylight to light a statue is the Charioteer in Delphi (Case Study pp. 170–171).

Daylight by its nature gives meaning and aids our understanding of a shape or space by its directional flow; a meaning which is emphasized even further by the addition of direct sunlight.

Interior spaces are judged to be pleasant, bright or gloomy as a result of the effects of modelling and interiors are judged by the way in which the spaces and the objects within them are seen during the day to be natural, or accord to our experience of the natural world.

London Metropolitan University

The charioteer statue at Delphi, daylit (See Case Study pp. 170–171)

ORIENTATION

The importance of orientation in a building must be considered at the outset, when the architect is planning the location of the building on the site, the aim being to ensure the maximum availability of useful natural light and sunlight to the interior.

There may of course be severe restrictions where the building is set into a rigid street pattern, or where there are severe external obstructions; but even in these circumstances the best use of the daylighting available should be considered. The architect will have the greatest flexibility to get the building orientation right on a greenfield site, where he can plan the site layout to take advantage of the sun path and the availability of the daylight.

Taking an example from residential buildings in the northern hemisphere, and using the simple fact that the sun rises in the east and sets in the west, it would be normal to ensure that those rooms which might benefit most from early morning light, such as a kitchen, morning room or even bedrooms, are placed on the east side, whilst those more likely to be used in the afternoon or evening such as living rooms face south or west.

There will of course be debate about the desirability of selecting a specific orientation for a particular use of room and it will be up to the architect to discuss this with his client, and there may also be conflict with the orientation of a room when associated with the ability to enjoy a particular view.

As with all architecture a compromise will need to be established which best fits the needs of the interior function. What is essential is that the orientation of a building and the interior layout takes most advantage of the daylight available and is a factor taken into consideration at the outset of the building design.

Each architectural programme whether an office, school or church, will have its own specific needs of orientation, and this is of special significance where the interior function is one requiring the inhabitants to sit in fixed positions, often the case in offices or classrooms.

Another aspect of orientation and one where the mere presence of daylighting is reassuring, is the subconscious desire of people when inside a building to keep in touch with the outside world, whether to know the time of day or the nature of the weather. An example of this might be taken from the modern shopping centre. The Victorians had got it right when they introduced overhead daylighting from domes or barrel vaults to their shopping arcades. But in the 1960s many of our early shopping centres cut out daylight altogether, leading to people finding it difficult to negotiate their way around or to find the exits.

City Plaza, Hong Kong

In one large shopping centre built in Hong Kong in the 1970s where daylight had been eliminated, visitors felt so disorientated that extreme measures had to be taken; whilst at City Plaza, another shopping centre of similar size where daylight had been provided over much of the multistorey space, it was an immediate success.

There is little likelihood that any shopping centre built now would not be daylit, there is a public demand for natural light in large open areas used by the public during the day and whilst the individual shop may be lit with artificial light to enhance the goods on sale, the public areas will assist orientation by the provision of daylight. At night the whole atmosphere will change, contributing to the variety we associate with the high street shop with artificial light taking over after dark.

Harlequin Centre, Watford. Overhead daylight provides orientation in an area without an external view

SUNLIGHT EFFECT

In his major work *Sunlight as Formgiver for Architecture*, Bill Lam asks the question ... The Sun: Problem or Opportunity? and then proceeds to show how the answer can really be both, depending very much on the location of the building. Clearly in hot climates where the sun is overhead for much of the day the problem is not so much one of welcome, but of exclusion.

In Britain where the sun is all too rare the answer must clearly be one of welcome, and an early decison when an architect is planning the orientation of his building is to encourage the entry of sunlight. Sunlight adds to the overall level of light when it is available, and adds to those other environmental factors such as variety and change, modelling and the creation of delight. There is a different level of experience when getting up in the morning to a sunlit world, as experienced from the interior of a building, and it is important that an element of sunlight is available for some part of the day.

Architects have used the sunlight effect in buildings to create a specific atmosphere, as for example the shafts of light entering the south side of our great cathedrals; and on a much smaller scale the use in houses of daylight and sunlight entry from above to provide necessary functional light to interior areas, where otherwise little natural light would be available.

The impression of sunlight is also important seen from windows which themselves admit no sunlight, but where the view of a sunlit landscape or buildings may be enjoyed. Whenever sunlight is available there is a strong desire to perceive it, and disappointment when it is unnecessarily excluded.

There is of course the obverse side associated with heat gain and glare, depending upon the orientation of the glazing, and whether people working in a building are confined to a fixed position. The effects of direct sunlight can be a disadvantage. Some control may be required in certain circumstances at certain times of year, and as far as heat gain is concerned this is best done beyond the window, and is of a sufficiently

Pathway in Hertfordshire. Daylight orientation in countryside.

flexible nature to be available only when required, or if fixed, not to inhibit the view.

One of the methods adopted to control the glare effect is to use forms of glazing which cut down light transmission; these need to be treated with care to avoid the impression that the interior of a building is permanently dim, and some glazing is available which reacts to the external light available, only cutting down the light when the sunlight is too bright, and might cause glare.

To sum up, the need for the admission of sunlight is important, the architect must consider this as a first requirement in planning the location and layout of the building, but in certain circumstances controls will be needed.

COLOUR

Whilst the colour of daylight will vary from morning to evening, and with changes in the sky and weather patterns; it is always regarded as the reference by which colour is judged . . . daylight is regarded as 'real colour.'

In early stores, such as Harrods, voids were opened in the roof to admit daylight to sales areas below; whereas for some years this was ignored. There were several reasons for this, not least being that it was considered that means of artificial light were more suitable for display, to show off the goods 'in a better light.'

This tended to ignore the environmental advantages of daylight and natural colour, and this has since been recognized in many new large shopping areas, where the entry of daylight is encouraged for the provision of environmental light to the store, but where for display purposes artificial light may be introduced locally to enhance the product.

The old concept of 'taking something to the light', by which was meant daylight, may be less of a necessity if the environmental light gives natural colour; whilst from the point of view of the shop worker who must remain in the same environment all day the advantage of natural light is obvious.

Staircase at Berkeley, USA. Shadow pattern conflict

Sunlight and shadow

Courtyard Mallorca. Sunlight and Shadow

DP Archive

NEC Birmingham. Sunlight and Shadow

DP Archive

The same applies to office buildings, where people tend to have to stay in the same atmosphere all day; if workers are too far from a window and the impression of natural light is greatly reduced, there is a sense of dissatisfaction. This is recognized by management, ensuring that for a part of the working day, for example during coffee breaks or in the office dining room, there is access to daylight, a change of environment.

It is generally recognized that vision is enhanced by good contrast, and that the natural colour of daylight increases contrast; it is argued that this permits lower illumination levels, whilst increasing visibility[1].

---

[1]*The Design of Lighting*. Peter Tregenza and David Loe

IMPORTANCE OF VIEW

Although listed last amongst the environmental factors, the question of view is of special importance. The view out from the window is our contact with the world outside; it provides the information, which for reasons already mentioned, allows us to experience the time of day, changes in the weather, sunlight and the seasons.

Field of Rape, Hertfordshire. Natural colour

At one level, a view satisfies the physiological need for the adaptation and readaptation of the eye to distance, providing a visual rest centre. For this reason any view is better than no view, whilst clearly some views will be better than others. At a different level the importance of a view has been recognized in research to show that a patient in hospital will recover more quickly where a window with a view is available.

The content of a view is clearly of importance, and it is the information it provides which will determine its success. A view out to a blank wall may be better than nothing but a view out to open countryside, or a garden will be a different order of experience.

Various views have been analysed in terms of the information obtained, depending upon the height of the window. In tall buildings the view may consist entirely of the sky when seen from the interior of the space, whilst at lower levels the experience of the ground scene becomes of more importance.

The quality of the exterior view will depend upon the surroundings of the building, and the height at which it is experienced, but it is of importance that where a view is available it should be exploited. There will be instances in large building complexes where internal views from one part of the interior to another may be had; these will provide the visual rest centres to satisfy the physiological requirement, but unless there are views to daylit areas they will lack the amenities of change, variety and modelling which inform the natural scene outdoors.

The architect should take the question of view into consideration when planning his building, and when planning the location and detail of the windows. Some of the finest windows were those of the eighteenth century in Britain where the refinement of detail of the glazing bar ensured that the daylight was captured by the bar, led round it, not impeding the view. This is less necessary today since the size of glass available is such as to allow large areas of see-through glazing, with no need for horizontal obstruction.

Interior of a greenhouse at Kew Gardens. Lit by daylight

There are some architectural programmes where it is thought that a view out may lead to a lack of concentration, as in a school classroom. It was the author's experience that classrooms in his school in the 1930s had windows at high level, precluding a view out; a view which prevailed until the new school building programmes of the 1960s. Other building programmes, such as churches or factories, also tend to ignore the need for a view, and it is perhaps understandable in a building used only for a short space of time, that the question of view doesn't figure large in the architect's priorities, and in the case of the daylit factory it would be reasonable to suppose that there might be dangers associated with lack of concentration when working with potentially dangerous machinery if a view out were provided.

The question of 'view-out' is necessarily associated with 'view-in' raising the question of privacy, which in certain circumstances may be deemed to be of importance. During the day this will generally not be a problem, as the level of daylight outside will be greater than that within,

Concourse at Abu Dhabi Airport. Artificial colour

inhibiting the view-in but at night the situation will be reversed, and it may be necessary to resort to some form of blind or curtain, which can have the desirable effect of ensuring that the window is not seen as a black hole from the interior at night.

HEALTH

Daylight has long been associated with health, and in Dr Hobday's book, *The Healing Sun*, he reminds us of the work of Vitruvius in the first century BC with his ten books on architecture. Among the classic principles of harmony proportion and symmetry, as Vitruvius set out,

View out of window to fountain at Waddesden

View to Garden from study in a private house. House of Justin De Syllas (Case Study pp. 108–111)

The Street at Waterside BA HQ. Internal views

View from roof top restaurant at Peter Jones store

he emphasized that architects should select healthy sites for their buildings, and that careful design of buildings prevented illness. It was clear that the healthy site was one which was oriented to permit the introduction of natural light. Vitruvius was the first to study the qualitative and quantitative aspects of daylight, proposing explicit rules to assess whether an interior is well daylit.

We may have moved a great deal further than this now, but poor daylighting and the lack of sunlight is said to be responsible for what is described as 'Seasonal Affected Disorder' or SAD, which affects a large number of people at certain times of the year due to the lack of sunlight. It is not a coincidence that given the choice, people prefer to work in daylight, and choose to locate close to a window. The presence of natural light at times when it is available in a building, is an important environmental consideration.

It is often forgotten that people are the major asset and expense of a company. To get relative costs into perspective, the annual lighting costs of a person in an office can be the equivalent to only 3–4 hours salary. If staff are visually impaired through inadequate working conditions and poor lighting, their productivity will deteriorate and output may decline on a scale far greater than the gains which might occur from the installation of more energy efficient (but less user friendly) lighting.

Poor lighting can affect workers' health, badly designed or poorly maintained lighting can cause stress and lead to various forms of complaint, eye discomfort, vision or posture. Dry or itching eyes, migraines, aches, pains and other symptoms, often known as Sick Building Syndrome, can be caused by poor or inappropriate lighting installations. A purely energy efficient approach to workplace lighting, which pays little or no attention to user comfort, could turn out to be both ugly and ineffective.

It would be a mistake to adopt energy efficiency as the principal measure of good lighting, and whilst important, it should be balanced against those other factors leading to a comfortable and pleasant environment.

Daylit Health Spa at Hotel in Abu Dhabi

3 Windows

Windowshapes . . . rooflights . . . atriums . . . glazing . . . high tech glazing . . . window openings . . . symbolism . . . solar shading . . . privacy . . . innovative systems . . . the future

The window is an opening in a wall or side of a building admitting light and often air to the interior. Early windows were developed before the introduction of glass, so initially windows were left open to the external atmosphere, or filled by some form of closure to minimize the heat loss at night. The more sophisticated buildings would have had thin slabs of marble, mica or oiled paper for this purpose.

In mediaeval times wooden shutters were installed on the interior, and these were left open or closed to regulate the light and air. With the introduction of glass, used first in small panes in Roman architecture, the window as we know it today had its beginnings. The concept of small panes of glass, divided by bronze or later lead divisions, as used in early buildings dies hard and window manufacturers still offer these as

Smallhythe Place, Sussex.

DP Archive

Carpenters' shop, Weald and Downland Museum

Splayed recess

alternatives to fully glazed windows in new domestic work, however inappropriate they may appear.

Windows can broadly be divided into two main types, first the window set in the side walls of a building, and second the opening light set into the roof, generally known as rooflights.

The daylight penetration from side windows will depend upon the ceiling height, and in early buildings where the ceiling heights were low, the penetration of daylight into the building was severely limited ... with the design of the important houses of the seventeenth and eighteenth centuries the ceiling heights were raised and daylight was able to reach further into the interiors. However as buildings became grander, even

Clerestories, York Minster

Soane Museum frontage

Georgian window, Soane museum

Orange Operational facility

Les Shipsides

this was not enough, and the concept of the rooflight was developed to introduce daylight into interiors far from the side windows.

Illustrations of some window types indicate the variety of window shapes that have evolved over the centuries, set into the vertical sides of buildings.

The horizontal window is perhaps the most well known of all, starting as it did in mediaeval times, limited by the construction methods of the day. It is still much used in today's domestic architecture. Provided the horizontal window is placed high in the wall the daylighting will penetrate well into the space, but other features of the window need to be considered, such as the view out which will be prejudiced where the cill is too high.

A logical development of this type is where the horizontal window extends the entire length of the external wall, a device used in nineteenth century industrial buildings to provide even and sufficient light for machine operators. This type of window required new structural techniques to overcome the need for vertical support to the structure above.

Yet a further example is the clerestorey; found mainly in tall buildings such as churches, generally associated with other forms of window at lower level to provide the main daylight. Clerestoreys are placed at high level to assist in getting daylight further into the interior and to light the roof structure.

A logical development of the extended horizontal window, is the floor to ceiling window; as structural techniques were perfected, this type of window has become almost universal in some types of architectural programme such as the office. The 1930s saw the innovation of the wrap around corner window as further structural techniques were made possible.

DP Archive

City Hall, London. Interior/exterior

Finally and in no chronological order comes the vertical window. Vertical windows were popular from the fourteenth century, having perhaps their most glorious period in the eighteenth century, when the Georgian window with its sophisticated detailing was almost universal. Tall windows, set apart by masonry at intervals, provided a simple structural solution and this formed the pattern of development in residential and other building types for several centuries.

The window can be said to be the most important architectural feature of a building; this is the first experience that a visitor will have when seeing the building for the first time, and architects have naturally considered the form of the window and its relationship to the exterior to be vital.

Three buildings on London's Embankment

The illlustrations of these buildings along the Embankment illustrate three different approaches to fenestration. All buildings are of the twentieth century. The first, on the left, shows the more traditional separate windows, whilst that in the middle is an example of the continuous horizontal window, where the individual floors are expressed as important horizontal bands. The building on the right is the further development where the window becomes a subsidiary part of the external cladding, for a total glass façade. The appearance of the buildings says little about the success of the daylighting, it says more about architectural fashion.

ROOFLIGHTS

Whilst rooflights could properly have been said to have started with the central courtyards or atria of the Roman house, these were open to the sky and rain; and despite providing daylight to the surrounding dwelling space, would not have modified the exterior climate in the manner of a roof light.

The rooflight by definition permits daylight to enter from above through a glazed opening in the roof protecting the interior from wind and weather. The early rooflights were perceived either as domes such as that at Chiswick House with ordinary windows in the sides allowing in the daylight, but by the nineteenth century structural techniques had developed sufficiently to allow fully glazed barrel vaults or glazed domes to be placed above areas of building remote from the side walls and the proximity of windows. Examples of nineteenth century shopping malls still exist today where these overhead lights permit daylight to reach deep into the interior of buildings.

Much innovation was used in the nature of these rooflights, and it is of interest to study the section of the Soane Museum, to see the many different shapes and sizes of overhead light Soane devised to introduce daylight to the different spaces, in what was at the time his private house.

Shopping Centre in Leeds. Barrel vaulted rooflight

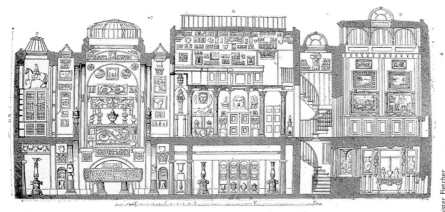

16. Section through the Museum, 1827

Section through the Soane Museum

By the twentieth century the use of rooflights had been reduced almost entirely to industrial buildings, and the CIBSE Lighting Guide LG10, 'Daylighting and Window Design' (published October 1999) illustrates a number of different types, the most common of which were the shed roof, the sawtooth, and the monitor.

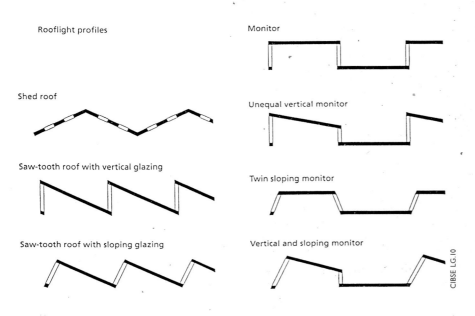

Rooflight profiles

Shed roof

Saw-tooth roof with vertical glazing

Saw-tooth roof with sloping glazing

Monitor

Unequal vertical monitor

Twin sloping monitor

Vertical and sloping monitor

CIBSE LG.10

Rooflight profiles

The advantages and disadvantages are set out in CIBSE LG10 indicating that the original shed roof, the cheapest solution, has serious defects and is unlikely to be used today; whilst the many different forms of monitor roof can be adapted to fit most roof situations to solve the daylighting problems below.

New roof forms are still being developed for the admission of daylight to large open areas not restricted to industrial buildings … from supermarkets to universities and swimming pools. An excellent example of an early solution to a factory in which the services are rationalized and placed inside ducts which are a part of the overall roof structure and do not obstruct the daylight is shown in *Lighting Modern Buildings* pp. 138/9, the York Shipley Factory; whilst the roof design for the Sainsbury Supermarket in Greenwich (Case Study pp. 164/167) shows an elegant solution to the roof form, providing a high level of daylight to the store.

ATRIA

Whilst the word atrium started as the central court of a Roman house, admitting light and air to the surrounding dwelling space, the word has taken on a wider meaning as described in the CIBSE LG10 daylight and window design.

> 'An interior light space enclosed on two or more sides by the walls of a building, and daylit from a roof of transparent or translucent material and, sometimes, from glazed ends or sides. It permits the entry of light to the other interior spaces, linked to it by glazed or unglazed openings.'

The atrium is therefore a further development of the dome or vault allowing daylight into the central areas of the great houses. The modern atrium will be covered by a glazed skylight, which, whilst slightly reducing the amount of daylight, monitors the external atmosphere keeping out the rain, whilst contributing to ventilation, and reducing the necessity for air-conditioning.

The square atrium at Borax which may be compared with the 'street' at the BA Headquarters at Waterside (see p. 17)

DP Archive

The proportions of the atrium and the reflective capacity of the enclosing wall surfaces are critical, and those atria which are wide in relation to their height, will perform better than taller, narrower spaces in ensuring that daylight reaches the lower levels. Having said this, the elongated atrium, which can act as an internal street at the low level, has proved successful in providing the impression of a daylit interior, even if due to its height the measured level of daylight at the lowest level will be much reduced.

In order to optimize the daylight at the lower levels one method is to set back the floor plans at the higher levels to maximize the direct view of the sky at the lower; but this has planning limitations and economic implications for the building owner.

Summarizing the advantages of atrium design

First, the human advantages: by getting daylight into the centre of deep plan buildings, this provides the occupants with a sense of orientation, information on the time, weather and the world outside the building; together with a sense of space and expansive views which may compensate for the lack of external views from the building.

Second, the environmental advantages: there is a potential for savings of energy, assistance with the problems of ventilation, and a reduction in the need for air-conditioning. Depending upon the orientation and detail of the rooflight there may be a need for some solar shading.

On balance the advantages outweigh the disadvantages, as over the life of the building the cost of the people who work there greatly exceeds those of its construction, and the work environment is crucial.

Glazing

There is now a large amount of alternative glazing for windows, and it is necessary for the architect, in conjunction with his services consultant, to write a detailed performance specification; this must include the orientation of the window, its thermal and acoustic characteristics, together with its capacity for solar shading. This is of course in addition to the main function of the window which is the admission of daylight and the introduction of the view to outside. Further factors which may need to be taken into account, are whether it is thought desirable to have windows which open or are fixed, and its relationship to ventilation.

But here our concern is with the types of glazing which are available. As already stated the main purpose of a window is for the admission of daylight, and associated with this the view to the exterior.

Glazing types which reduce the impression of daylight significantly, darken both the interior, and the view, whilst the view from the outside towards the building makes the façade look black. It is only when comparisons are made between the view through a clear glass window and one with a modifying glass that reduces the daylight, that the results create disappointment ... it is true to say that it is human nature to appreciate the natural environment, with all its variations of colour, light and shade.

This is particularly true of residential properties where some form of dark glass has been applied to the façade, giving the impression of a dull day seen from the interior, as compared to the view through a clear window.

There are basically three main types of glazing as follows.

1. Clear glazing

This can be single sheet, double or triple glazed or alternatively a 'thick' glass, but the more sheets or the greater the thickness of glass the more the daylight will be diminished, although the impression of the colour of the exterior will still be perceived as natural.

Clear glass whilst allowing a high transmission of daylight, will at the same time and on certain building façades allow a high transmission of solar radiation. It is this fact that has led to the development of the more high-tech glasses designed to reduce solar gain, with their consequent loss of daylight transmission. Other means such as interplane blinds, located between the panes of glass, may present a solution. These would only need to to be installed on façades subject to solar gain and then only activated when required.

2. Tinted glass

This is of two types: the first where the clear glass is itself modified in such a way as to produce different radiant heat transmission character-istics, therefore the thicker the glass the lower the transmission of daylight, and the greater the control of radiant heat from sunlight.

The second type of glasses are those coated with microscopically thin layers of metallic oxides which reflect the heat away and out of the building. These coatings are applied to the inside layer of glass generally in association with other panes in a sealed double glazed unit as a protection, since on their own they would be vulnerable to damage.

These coated glasses can be designed to have high daylight transmis-sion, due to the very thin layer of reflective material; so that they almost give the appearance of clear glass, and do not suffer from the objections raised by tinted glasses which reduce the daylight significantly. Additionally they do not obstruct the view; however they do have cost implications, and should only be used where the specification demands it. Highly reflective glasses are available, but need to be used with care to avoid the danger of glare to other buildings or motorists.

3. Miscellaneous glazing

A number of different types of glazing are placed in this category, largely because they cannot be lumped together into a single category; they consist of the following:

Patterned glass, wired glass, laminated glasses and glass blocks.

Patterned glass

Any number of patterns can be rolled into semi-molten glass, to provide decorative or diffusing sheets for various purposes, though rarely for windows, since their capacity for light transmission will be modified.

Wired glass

A similar process is used for the manufacture of wired glass, where a wire mesh is sandwiched within the thickness of the glass. This used generally in security situations, and sometimes as a protection to vulnerable skylights.

Laminated glasses

Similar methods of manufacture are used for laminating sheets of plastic between sheets of glass, again used for security reasons as resistance to impact. These reduce the transmission of daylight.

In museums where exhibits are exposed to daylight, it will be necessary to control the entry of UV light. This may be done by the use of laminated glasses, where UV absorbing filters can be laminated between the sheets of clear glass.

Glass blocks

These were a popular form of glass wall in the 1930s, having thermal characteristics due to the hollow nature of the blocks, which, because of their structural nature are still in use today for the introduction of daylight into new buildings, but special openings will be required to provide a view.

Finsbury Health Centre. The foyer

DP Archive

High tech glazing

There are a number of glazing types which fall into this category, the most advanced of which are the photovoltaics, where the glass itself is designed to generate electricity from solar radiation on south facing exposures, which can then be used within the building to reduce the energy required for the artificial lighting. Some buildings already use this method, and the UK Government is now putting research money into its further development. (See Doxford International Building Park. Lighting Modern Buildings. Case No 11, pp. 124/5).

Two other types of high tech glass deserve mention, but are not at present economically viable for general use in buildings.

The first are the photochromic glasses, which respond directly to an environmental stimulus (temperature or light) rather like the special sunglasses which are already available which alter their transmission factor depending upon the brightness of the ambient light; alternatively there are the electrochromic glasses designed to respond indirectly by the application of an electrical current which alters their visual and thermal characteristics. These glasses are still at the experimental stage, but are likely to be developed further to a point where they may become viable.

The choice of glazing in a large complex is one of the greatest importance, having implications both on first cost, and the cost in use of the project.

WINDOW DETAILS

The Georgian window developed in the eighteenth century satisfied all the known criteria at the time. It admitted unadulterated daylight, it provided ventilation when required, and it could be controlled by internal shutters, providing additional security. The splay at the sides (and sometimes at the cill as well) together with the careful detailing of the glazing bars, assisted in balancing the brightness between the inside of the room and the outside. However it did little for thermal insulation, and on sunny elevations problems of solar gain and the possibility of glare, were considered less important at the time.

Windows have developed a long way from this point, from the standard horizontal or vertical windows set into the side walls of the majority of residential properties, to the window walls commonly found in modern office blocks. The Georgian window, however, provides some lessons which have apparently not been learnt today, mostly to do with the subtlety of the detailing.

Extension to Boxmoor church

Window with symbolic cross. Compare with the windows of the original church, having their own symbolism

1. To assist with modern methods of production, the timber sections used for dividing the opening parts from the fixed glazed areas, tend to be heavy, interrupting the view out, particularly where they cross the sight lines of those inside.

2. Where glazing bars are required, between the different glazed areas they are often very heavy, and where in the Georgian window the detailing would have allowed the light to flow around the bar, reducing its apparent size, the modern glazing bar tends to create unsatisfactory shadows within and a barrier to the view, further reducing the amount of daylight available.

3. The use of splayed sides between the window and the wall, to balance the brightness of the window seen against the brightness of the interior of the room has almost been forgotten, a lesson learnt in our mediaeval churches, and which is equally relevant today; the use of the splay to conceal security shutters may however not be required. This is of course not to deny the advantages of the modern domestic window, in terms of both thermal and acoustic capacity, with the introduction of double glazing.

Whilst the majority of windows are of the type discussed, set into walls at intervals, either horizontal or vertical, each having their own characteristics in determining the quality of daylight entering the room. It is more likely that wall-to-wall windows will be used in modern office blocks, and these will have their own structural detailing; for example there may be no need to have horizontal divisions since the glass sizes will generally be able to stretch between the cill and the ceiling level or spandrel, whilst the divisions between the wide panes of glass horizontally can be minimized to avoid the break-up of the view.

It will however be important to consider the junction at the point where the window meets a wall at right angles at a major subdivision of the space, or the end of the building; here the reflection factor of the wall

Corbusiers church in Ronchamp. Detail of a window where symbolism characterizes the interior

View of the exterior

needs to be kept high, to avoid a conflict of brightness. Alternatively the architect may wish to break up the elevation of his building, by the introduction of structural elements which articulate the perimeter of the façade. In such cases the wide horizontal windows located between the vertical structures might be treated in the same manner as the splays of the more traditional building. The window elevations of buildings need to be carefully considered when related to the orientation of the façades, with care taken to provide solutions to any exposure where there is a need for solar shading and protection from glare.

Windows can provide a degree of symbolism; this was apparent on the type of window used for Anglican churches, which from frequent use become symbolic of this type of church. Many examples exist of symbolism in the windows of churches, not least in the stained glass infilling. A modern example of symbolism in a new extension to an Anglican church in Boxmoor, where it is clear that the Christian cross is visible; this may be compared with the original windows.

SOLAR SHADING

This is a subject where expert advice should be sought. There are many different forms of solar shading; each has its own characteristics, advantages and disadvantages, and the architect must be sure of the criteria that should be taken into account when determining the nature of the shading required and whether some form of adjustability is desirable.

The BRE pamphlet 'Solar Shading of Buildings' states that the principal reasons for needing shading are as follows:

1. To reduce the effect of heat gain from the sun
2. To cut down sun glare experienced through the windows
3. The provision of privacy. This will not normally be a requirement, but it may be important in certain circumstances.

1.   Reduction of heat gain from the sun

At some times of the year this may be of the greatest importance, but its need will not be permanent; for certain times of the year the heat gain may be welcome.

The problem is most acute on South facing exposures, but there may be special conditions in the building such as abnormally high internal heat gains, or where the building has to be kept at a low temperature.

Since once the heat gain is within the building envelope, it is difficult to control, the shading system which stops the heat from getting in in the first place ... the external system ... will be better. When contemplating external shading, it is important to bear in mind the question of structural stability and the need for periodic cleaning.

2.   Reduction of sun glare

Glare may result from a direct view of the sun, by reflection from some outside source such as the building opposite a North facing exposure, or by reflection from items inside the building; most noticeably from items which are the object of attention, such as a business machine or computer. Glare, unlike heat, can be controlled easily from within the building.

3.   Provision of privacy

This is really the 'net curtain' solution, if it is needed at all. Some form of translucent material which lets through the maximum amount of daylight, but breaks up the internal image seen from the outside. This is less important during the day when the light ouside exceeds that within and there is no disadvantage in placing the diffusing material on the inside of the window. In certain security situations special materials have been developed which in addition to the provision of privacy, capture the shards of glass which occur when a window is broken

Solar shading solutions can broadly be divided into the following three types:

1   External shading
2   Internal shading
3   Alternative glazing

(*Note.* The BRE pamphlet further lists as a solution the reduction in the area of glazing, comparing this with the loss of daylight associated with the use of some form of tinted 'sun control' glazing. On the basis that the window areas have been calculated correctly in the first place, this must reduce the daylight available, and for this reason has not been included.)

I.   External shading

The following methods are available: Overhangs and canopies, light shelves, fixed and movable louvres, shutters, vertical fins, deep window reveals, egg-crate baffles, and roller blinds.

When choosing a method of external shading, the most crucial decision that must be taken is the long-term viability of the hardware involved, associated with the climatic conditions which will be experienced on site; there is also the architect's preoccupation with the exterior appearance of the building with which the former is associated.

Whilst it is best to control the heat gain before it enters the building by external means, any method of external shading can be vulnerable, and the cost and long-term viability of the method employed must be established. Comparisons should be made with internal shading methods, to establish whether the gains in heat control are sufficient to warrant what will initially be expensive, and possibly a long-term maintenance problem.

The following list of shading types are some of the options available, each having their own advantages and disadvantages; although the visual appearance of each type may have more influence with tbe architect as to how he sees the impact on the elevation of the building:

Overhangs and canopies
Continental shutters, and awnings
Light shelves
Fixed and movable louvres
Egg-crate louvres
External roller blinds
Brise soleil

2.   Internal shading

It must be recognized that any form of shading within the building envelope is bound to be less efficient as a control of heat gain than an external device, since the heat which is generated has already entered the building, and is more difficult to extract; however the type of shade will be less vulnerable than that outside, will be easier to maintain and to clean, so that an overall view must take into account all the factors in coming to a decision. If of course it is not possible to control the solar gain sufficiently inside, then other means will have to be adopted.

The most common form of control and one used almost universally in residential building, is the curtain, and provided these are carefully designed, perhaps with a reflective lining to reduce the solar gain when pulled across the opening (whilst at night they can keep out the cold) can be perfectly satisfactory in our temperate climate … indeed we welcome the sun on all but the exceptional day.

A more flexible form of control is the venetian blind, which has the advantage of adjustability in that it can be raised when not required for sun control, to permit maximum daylight entry.

The demise of this excellent tool has been predicted for many years, but it survives, offering excellent glare control, can be motorized when used in large office projects, can be incorporated within panes of glass to protect it from damage, and specialist versions are available where the tilt of the blades can be varied to enable the top of the blind to reflect light up to the ceiling of a room, whilst the lower blades control the sunlight by reflecting it away from the building. A further advantage of the venetian blind is that the surface design of the horizontal slats can be varied to meet the individual requirements of the building.

The obvious advantage of the venetian blind is that it can and should be raised when not needed for sun control; the problem is that once lowered it tends to be left in the closed position. A procedure should be adopted to ensure that their use is optimized and a simple solution might be for the office cleaners to open the blinds to ensure that each day starts with them open to admit the maximum daylight. Venetian blinds have a lot of life in them yet .

Other types of blind are also available, the vertical hung louvre blind where the louvre slats can be rotated, or moved to one side offer flexibility, provide privacy, and together with roller blinds and those of other materials can provide low-cost solutions in the domestic situation.

The heat gain from the sun can be controlled by the type of glass used, various options being available, First there are the low emissivity glazings, developments in this field continue, and the thermal properties of the glass can now be tailored to give good solar control. Their big advantage is that they admit higher levels of daylight than the original tinted versions, and can control heat loss.

Prismatic glazing panels have also proved useful; these are limited to small panels of prismatic glazing which, when attached to high level rooflights, can allow daylight to enter, but redirects the sunlight on to the ceiling of the space, or excludes it altogether.

Finally there are the high tech glazings already referred to under the glazings available for windows. These include the following:

- Electrochromic and liquid crystal glazings, which can be made to darken on application of an electric current
- Photochromic glass, which darkens when sunlight falls on it
- Thermochromic glass which alters its transmission value on the introduction of heat.

None of the latter is in the mainstream of development, and it is unlikely that these will have a major impact for some years.

INNOVATIVE DAYLIGHTING SYSTEMS

In 1998 Paul Littlefair of the BRE wrote a seminal paper on this subject, listing as its aims: to improve the distribution of daylight in a space and to control direct sunlight.

Of the various methods none can be said to have achieved a universal application, but each has a specific use and is worthy of mention.

Mirrors. There are many ways in which the interaction of light or sunlight with a mirrored surface can be used for reflection. From the use of a large hand-held mirror to throw light into the dark recesses of a renaissance church for the delight of visitors, to the fixed mirrored louvres which may be related to vertical windows, installed to direct light upwards to a ceiling; alternatively there are those which, when related to glazed openings in a roof, can project light downwards to the interior (see Case Study of the Central United Methodist Church in Wisconsin pp. 142–143). These tend to be specialist solutions requiring the mirror to be controlled by a motorized tracking system or heliostat ... not for general application.

Prismatic glazing. The principle is to use methods of refraction of light, rather than reflection. Whilst this method can be applied to vertical windows, they are perhaps more successful when associated with systems of rooflight, a good example being Richard Rogers' redevelopment of Billingsgate fish market to a modern computer centre (see *Lighting Historic Buildings*, p. 64) where sunlight is refracted away from the occupants to eliminate glare, whilst allowing daylight to the space below. As these have only a limited application they are expensive.

Light shelves. It is possible by means of comparatively inexpensive building construction, to provide light shelves. These have already been mentioned in terms of solar shading, but they are useful also to provide a view window below the light shelf, with the light above reflected to the ceiling to redistribute daylight further into the room. It must be recognized that light shelves do not increase the daylight factors in a room, but they alter the distribution, assisting in getting light further towards the back of the room so that uniformity is improved. Light shelves are relatively cheap to install, and are less subject to damage than those used externally, but do require cleaning on a regular basis.

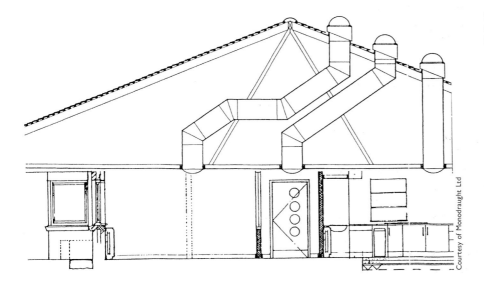

Section illustrating the passage of light pipes through a roof to provide daylight to a top floor room

Courtesy of Monodraught Ltd

Light pipes. Of all the methods of innovative daylighting, the light pipe has had the most universal application. It is basically a method of rooflighting, which by means of association with reflective tubes, directs the light to a lower level. Whilst it can be employed to direct light through several floors, this has the disadvantage of locating the pipes through the upper floors, taking up useful floor space.

Light-pipe installations can be associated with a means of ventilation, and also with sources of artificial light which take over after dark or when the daylight outside is insufficient, using a light control system. A particularly useful application has been in domestic buildings, where a light pipe can be directed to an area in the property, such as an upstairs landing, which otherwise might receive no daylight.

THE FUTURE

The design of 'the window' for a new building is of the first importance, not only because it will determine the appearance of the building, which it does, but because it is being asked to take a major role in the control of the building environment. It will be seen in the Case Studies to follow later in the book, that with the large increase in 'passive' buildings, it is the window which is at the leading edge of new development, development of which is as yet far from exhausted.

Courtesy of Monodraught Ltd

Photograph of typical light-pipe installation seen from inside the building

Colt 'Interactive' window

solar gain and glare.

External noise control

Mechanically controlled top ventilation window

External solar shading to reduce glare and heat gain

Light shelf

Individual hand control window

Internal solar blind

Courtesy of Studio E

To quote but one example of leading edge technology; a window designed by the architects Studio E. and developed to a practical stage by a manufacturer (Colt) as the 'interactive' window, shows an integrated approach to the environmental control of a building. It is of particular interest in that it does not demand the need for high tech glass solutions, using low-cost clear window glass.

The window is designed with the following criteria in mind:

1. The provision of daylight
2. To solve the problem of mechanically controlled building ventilation without creating draughts
3. To cater for adequate thermal insulation
4. To provide adequate sound insulation for normal circumstances.
5. To control solar gain and diminish sun and sky glare.

The features of the window allow individual control by occupants, accepted as an important characteristic in user satisfaction as is also the provision of a view, and can be tailored to suit individual environmental requirements. This is one example of the way in which industry is being led by architects to satisfy the needs of the environment.

Finally to quote from conclusions made at a conference at the RIBA in 1996:[1]

1. Windows are an essential element in building design, for the following reasons: change, colour, sunlight, modelling, orientation and view.
2. Window design, associated with the need to reduce energy in buildings, is leading towards high tech window design, where associated problems of ventilation, solar gain, glare and noise pollution suggest an integrated solution.
3. Air-conditioning, at least in this country, will become the exception rather than the rule.
4. There is a convergence between the provision of optimum visual and environmental conditions in building, and the world needs to come to terms with global warming, and the reduction of carbon dioxide emissions.

---

[1]'New Light on Windows.' Joint RIBA, BRE and CIBSE Seminar held at the RIBA, November 1996. Notes prepared by Derek Phillips, unpublished.

4 Energy

Reduction ... artificial light ... waste ... daylight ... control ... solar ... legislation

The introduction has stressed the need for a reduction in the use of energy in buildings; where the part played by a strategic role for daylighting can provide considerable savings in energy, and therefore of carbon dioxide emissions, leading to a reduction in greenhouse gases and ultimately a reduction in global warming.

This is now recognized by most governments, though there is still a reluctance to take sufficient measures to overcome the problems involved. The 'fossil fuels' which provide the bulk of the energy we use at present, are still thought of as cheap alternatives to action, ignoring the fact that coal, gas, and oil are a finite resource with limited life for the future, leading to a potential energy crisis.

Even where this is acknowledged, most governments have not put the necessary investment into alternative forms of energy, by developments in the fields of wave, wind or solar power. In the past there have been exceptions; one being in the development of hydroelectric power, where conditions have permitted and lucky the countries which have benefitted; another is in the use of solar power in certain countries which have exploited their natural environment; this is an area where a developing technology can play an important part in the future.

Nuclear power in the UK has not proved to be the answer, unlike early projections from journalists that energy would become almost free. The generation of energy by means of nuclear power stations, has become too expensive, added to the unsolved problems of the disposal of nuclear waste, to a point where it is unlikely using present technology for nuclear to provide the alternative to fossil fuels; the development of nuclear energy is more an issue for the environmentalist. There are countries, such as France, where a large part of their energy is derived from nuclear plants, but in the UK there does not at present seem to be either the will or the means.

The future therefore appears to lie in the development of alternative sources of energy, but the problem facing us today is in taking action to ameliorate the energy crisis as it exists.

The reduction in the use of energy in buildings has been identified as a major objective, of which electrical energy for lighting is a significant factor.

Lighting accounts for between a third and a half of the energy use in commercial buildings and significant savings in energy can be obtained where the positive use of daylight has been planned; associated with control systems, by means of 'daylight linking', natural light provides the major light source during the day with variable artificial light as back-up.

It will be found that in many of the Case Studies mentioned later in the book, daylight has provided the necessary amount of light for large parts of the building during the day, whilst providing the interior space with an overall impression of daylight, even in areas where the actual daylight factors may be relatively low, allowing light from artificial sources to be reduced, with consequent savings in energy.

ARTIFICIAL LIGHT

All forms of energy use in buildings should be analysed, related to the different needs of individual architectural programmes, to see where savings can be made; for example in homes, the use of the natural source has always been paramount during the day, so few savings can be made. At night however, developments in lamp technology have produced significantly more efficient artificial light sources and this is an area where, due to the large quantity of residential property, significant savings have yet to be made; moreover major energy savings in the home are to be found in the means of heating and insulation. Table 4.1 illustrates the different aspects of the main types of lamp, providing comparisons to assist the architect in making his choice. The different factors identified are those of efficacy, lamp life and colour, but other factors that must also be considered are those of cost and control.

It can be seen from the column under 'Lamp efficiency' that the favourite domestic lamp – Incandescent Tungsten – has an efficiency of only 7–14 Lm/watt, whilst the compact fluorescent (CFC) has an efficiency of between 40–87 Lm/watt. At present the CFC lamps cannot be dimmed economically, but there are many areas in homes, where dimming is not a requirement, and with satisfactory colour (2700 K) there is no reason not to take advantage of their long life and lower wattage.

The newer generation of lower-energy lamps such as the compact and T-5 linear fluorescent lamps can in many cases replace less efficient incandescent sources, which can be four to eight times more efficient; they can also have more than eight times longer lamp life. Used in conjunction with high frequency electronic control gear further reductions of 20 per cent in power consumption or energy savings can be made.

To realize these gains they must relate not only to the lamp, but also to matching this with the the correct luminaire or light fitting. It is no use simply fitting energy-efficient lamps into inappropriate luminaires, resulting in unsatisfactory installations; furthermore an energy efficient scheme demands regular, consistent and informed maintenance. It may also be cost effective in large installations to operate a system of 'bulk replacement' of lamps after a specific period irrespective of how many lamps may have failed.

In buildings for industrial use, no doubt savings may be possible in a rigorous investigation of the plant required to run industrial processes; but the area most likely to result in the greatest savings is in building services, and the greatest of these will be in the lighting, where daylight is the key.

Table 4.1 List of artificial light sources (originally printed in *Lit Environment*, pp. 92)

Lamp	Type	Lamp efficacy (Lm/W)*	Circuit efficacy (Lm/W)†	Rated average life (hr)‡	Wattages (W)	Colour temp (K)§	CIE group¶	CRI**
Incandescent	Tungsten Filament	7 to 14	7 to 14	1000	15 to 500	2700	1A	99
	HV Tung. Halogen	16 to 22	16 to 22	2000	25 to 2000	2800 to 3100	1A	99
	LV Tung. Halogen	12 to 27	10 to 25	2000 to 5000	5 to 150	2800 to 3100	1A	99
High Intensity discharge	Low pressure sodium (SOX)	100 to 200	85 to 166	16 000	18 to 180	N/A	N/A	N/A
Fluorescent tubes	Cold cathode	70	60	35 to 50 000	23 to 40 W/m	2800 to 5000	1A 2	55 to 65 85 to 90
	Halophosphate (T8 & T12)	32 to 86	13 to 77	10 000	15 to 125	3000 to 6500	2 to 3	c. 50
	Triphosphor (T5 & T8)	75 to 104	CCG: 48 to 82 ECG: 71 to 104	10 000 20 000	4 to 80	2700 to 6500	1A & 1B	85 to 98
Compact fluorescent twinbased	Triphosphor	40 to 87	CCG: 25 to 63 ECG: 33 to 74	8000 10 000	5 to 80	2700 to 5400	1A/1B 1B	85 to 98
Compact twinbased integral ballast	Triphosphor	30 to 65		15 000	3 to 23	2700	1B	85
Induction (fluorescent)	Triphosphor	65 to 86	60 to 80	60 000 (service life)	55 to 150	2700 to 4000	1B	85
High intensity discharge	High pressure sodium (SON)	75 to 150	60 to 140	28 000	50 to 1000	1900 to 2300	2 & 4	23 to 60
High intensity discharge (not recommended for new installations)	High pressure mercury (MBF)	32 to 60	25 to 56	24 000	50 to 1000	3300 to 4200	2 & 3	31 to 57
High intensity discharge	Metal halide (quartz) (ceramic)	60 to 120 87 to 95	44 to 115 71 to 82	3000 to 15 000 9000 to 12 000	35 to 2000 20 to 250	3000 to 6000 3000 to 4200	1A to 2 1A to 2	60 to 93 80 to 92

The Lit Environment, Osram Lighting, Updated to June 2003.

*Lamp efficacy indicates how well the lamp converts electrical power into light. It is always expressed in Lumens per Watt (Lm/W).

†Circuit efficacy takes into account the power losses of any control gear used to operate the lamps and is also expressed in Lm/W.

‡Rated average life is the time to which 50% of the lamps in an installation can be expected to have failed. For discharge and fluorescent lamps, the light output declines with burning hours and is generally more economic to group replace lamps before significant numbers of failures occur.

§Colour temperature is a measure of how 'warm' or 'cold' the light source appears. It is always expressed in Kelvin (K), e.g. warm white 3000 K, cool white 4000 K.

¶CIE colour rendering groups: A (excellent); 1B (very good); 2 (fairly good); 3 (satisfactory); 4 (poor).

**CIE colour rendering index: scale 0 to 100 where: 100 (excellent, e.g. natural daylight); 85 (very good, e.g. triphosphor tubes); 50 (fairly good, e.g. halophosphate tubes); 20 (poor, e.g. high pressure sodium lamps).

In the case of reflector lamps, where the light output is directional, luminous performance is generally expressed as *Intensity* – the unit of which is the *Candela (Cd) (1 Candela is an intensity produced by 1 Lumen emitting through unit solid angle, i.e. Steradian).*

One of the problems has been in the 'cheap energy policy' of Government; there may be other good reasons for this, but it has led in the past to a prodigal use of cheap energy, and it is only recently, with a looming energy crisis, that government has woken up to the vital need for savings to be made.

The first line of defence must be in avoidance of waste; for how many times do we pass a building with every light burning in the middle of the day when daylight is quite adequate, or after dark when the building is largely unoccupied. The total amount of energy wasted on a daily basis may not have been calculated, but it is considerable and arguably equals the amount of savings which can be made in other ways.

A particular example of this might be in transport buildings where artificial light is used all day irrespective of the level of daylight. There is no doubt a need for the level of daylight never to drop below the statutory design level, but this can be solved by adopting a system of control which links artificial light to the available daylight to ensure that the design level is maintained, whilst allowing significant reductions in the use of artificial light, which can be off for most of the day.

DAYLIGHT

The most obvious vehicle for energy saving in buildings is in exploiting the most abundant source of light available to us – daylight. Environmentally conscious assessments of building design are recognizing that daylight (and natural fresh air) is an important commodity and should be exploited to the full. Generally, people when asked, always prefer to work in a daylit environment. There is a growing acknowledgement that daylight produces positive effects, both physiological and psychological.

Forms of control are necessary to limit the potentially excessive levels of daylight, if it is not to become a nuisance, particularly on bright sunny days. A wide range of devices are available, from relatively inexpensive and simple internal blinds (roller, venetian etc.) through to high tech, computer-controlled heliodens, which track the sun.

Whilst a daylighting strategy will be needed in those buildings where a decision to provide air-conditioning has been adopted, it is in those buildings described as 'passive' where the greatest savings can be made.

A passive building is one in which the greatest use is made of natural resources ... natural light, solar power and ventilation derived from making use of the natural environment. Nature cannot provide all that is necessary, and even during the day there may well be a need for some additional energy use, in terms of lighting from artificial sources, or ventilation from some form of fan assistance, whilst in terms of solar power, this can be used to advantage.

CONTROLS

The careful introduction of lighting controls can ensure that the maximum use is made of the available daylight; so that the amount of artificial light is reduced automatically when all, or most of it, is no longer required to meet the design level.

The term 'daylight linking' has been used already, and this perhaps needs some explanation. It is used in the sense that the artificial lighting in a building is planned and controlled to support the natural light available during the day, to ensure that the combined lighting level meets the desired design level.

This can be done by planning the artificial lighting circuits so as to allow control by simple switching, so that those sources close to the window may be switched on only when required. Such unsophisticated means of control suffer from the human factor, in that once the artificial light close to the window is switched on it tends to be left on all day.

A more sophisticated method known as Permanent Supplementary Artificial Lighting (PSALI) was proposed by Prof. Hopkinson in the late 1950s; the first practical application of the technique being developed for the Esso Building (see *Lighting Modern Buildings*, p. 89) where there was dual switching for day and night, with the same lamp energy used throughout, but using the daylight available close to the windows to achieve the required design level when available. This still relied on the human factor to turn on the switch.

One of the greatest advances in the technology of lighting is in the development of modern control systems. These will be associated with light fittings which can react by photocell to the level of daylight available outside, enabling the design level to be maintained throughout the day, but offering considerable savings in energy.

The control system should be appropriate to the occupation of a space, and in a leaflet published by the British Research Establishment, Watford, UK, the following are identified.

1. Variable occupation. Occupants spend part of their time in the space, and part elsewhere, e.g. an office
2. Intermittent scheduled occupation, a meeting room
3. Full occupation, reception area
4. Intermittent occupation, storeroom areas.

Before deciding on the appropriate type of control it is useful to analyse the type of 'occupation' as above, as this may help to determine the nature of the control system.

It is unnecessary to dwell on the many types of control system, from 'intelligent' light fittings which react automatically to the ambient light level, adjusting the total light to meet the design level; to systems where each fitting may be controlled individually by an occupant to meet his or her needs by means of a manual controller, or groups of fittings which can be controlled by means of proximity switches, reacting to an occupant's presence.

It should be emphasized that the control system for a particular building or part of a building should be appropriate for its use, for example the control system for a church will be very different to that of an office or a factory. Each programme should be analysed and those areas of buildings where there is intermittent use, such as storage or warehouse, need to be provided with an appropriate control regime; if daylight is available, artificial light may not be required during the day at all, or by some means of occupancy or proximity switching.

Control systems are at the heart of energy savings, and daylight linking is an essential part of the solution, and may be linked into the BEMS (Building Energy Management System).

SOLAR

There are two distinct aspects to the question of the relationship of energy to the power of the sun. First there is the heat gain from the sun to those surfaces of the building which are insolated, for the most part on the south elevation but with some additions to east and west. This can be a useful addition to the heating of the building in the winter, but on the obverse side can produce overheating in the summer, which must be dealt with.

This however is not a matter to be dealt with under the heading of daylighting, it being more concerned with the heating and ventilation equation.

The second aspect, is very much one of daylighting; that of the use of the sun to generate power by means of solar panels or photovoltaics, this is an aspect of the relationship of the sun to energy, and a growing technology.

Despite the fact that we lack the climate to provide large quantities of solar power (as for example in Israel, where solar panels generating power are the rule on properties rather than the exception) the conversion of the sun's energy into useful power has been shown to be effective.

The building industry has a long way to go before the technology already available makes a substantial impact, but as the energy crisis becomes closer the means will be found (see *Lighting Modern Buildings*, Case Study No. 11. The Solar Office at Doxford International Business Park). It has been shown that some 30 per cent of the energy required for an office building can be provided by means of photovoltaic panels, provided that the orientation and construction of the building has been planned for it.

LEGISLATION

Up to the twenty-first century little effort had been made to limit the amount of energy used for the lighting of buildings by legislation; but a start was made by Part L of the Building Regulations of 1995, dealing with the conservation of fuel and power; this was a start to limiting the amount of energy used for lighting in buildings, and this coupled with the increased efficacy of the lamps and light fittings available from the lighting industry, had a material effect upon the energy demand.

In 2002, revisions to Part L made it a requirement to consider the need for 'energy efficient lighting' more seriously, and architects should be aware of the current regulations, which in themselves will no doubt be further updated and modified, to increase the need for further energy savings for the future.

The new Part L requires that 'Reasonable provision shall be made for the conservation of fuel and power in buildings other than dwellings, by ... installing in buildings artificial lighting systems which are designed and constructed to use no more fuel and power than is reasonable in the circumstances and making reasonable provision for controlling such systems'. There is some flexibility for lighting designers to comply with the regulations, and there is every reason for the spirit of the regulations to be wholeheartedly adopted.

The regulations are divided into two parts, the first (Part L1) dealing with dwellings, and the second (Part L2) with non-domestic buildings.

The latter takes in offices, industrial buildings and those of multi-residential use, such as hotels, hostels, old people's homes, hospitals and boarding schools. This is a very broad sweep of the majority of buildings, and architects should be aware of the implications ... it will not be sufficient to say that your client has demanded illumination levels of 1000 lux in a hotel foyer when to provide this level the amount of energy used is far in excess of the amount allowed for this type of space.

To give an example of the legislation the following is a quotation from Part L2: This refers to general lighting efficiency in office, industrial and storage buildings:

> 1.43 Electric lighting systems serving these buildings should be provided with 'reasonably efficient lamp/luminaire combinations.' A way of meeting the requirements would be to provide lighting with an initial efficacy averaged over the whole building of not less than 40 luminaire-lumens/circuit watt. This allows considerable design flexibility to vary the light output ratio of the luminaire, the luminous efficacy of the lamp, or the efficiency of the control gear.

A table of lamps which meet the criteria for general lighting follows:

Light source	Types and rating
High pressure sodium	All types and ratings
Metal halide	All types and ratings
Induction lighting	All types and ratings
Tubular fluorescent	26 mm. diam. (T8) lamps 16 mm. diam. (T5) lamps rated above 11 watts, provided with high efficiency control gear. 38 mm. diam. (T12) linear fluorescent lamps 2400 mm. in length.
Compact fluorescent (CFC)	All ratings above 11 watts
Other	Any type and rating with an efficiency greater than 50 lumens/ circuit watt.

Whilst this clearly precludes the use of tungsten lamps for general use, they can still be used in some areas which may demand their use; where the average over the whole building does not exceed the predetermined 40 luminaire-lumens/circuit watts ... there is flexibility.

A major difference in the new regulations is that they apply to display lighting, defined as 'lighting designed to highlight displays of exhibits or merchandise.' (Examples of display lighting are included in the Case Studies shown later, a good example being the Sainsbury Store in Greenwich (Case Study pp. 164–167) where high levels of environmental lighting are available during the day by the use of natural light from roof lights, but where in terms of Part L the overall energy use is below the limits of the requirements.)

Part L of the building regulations encourages the use of daylight linking, stressing the relationship between the available daylight, and controlled artificial light sources. Daylighting can be at the heart of energy savings in buildings, and whilst in the early twentieth century this was largely forgotten, at the beginning of the twenty-first it has been shown to be a key to the future.

SUMMARY

The CIE have published a set of guidelines for lighting design for energy conservation, which if adhered to will ensure the creation of a lit environment that is appropriate, energy conscious and that should satisfy both EEC and UK lighting directives. These are as follows:

1. Analyse the task in terms of difficulty, duration, criticality and location, to determine the lighting needs throughout a space, taking into account the visual differences among people due to age and other factors.
2. Design the lighting so as to provide the necesssary illiumination on the task in accordance with current recommendations.
3. Select the most efficient lamps appropriate to the type of lighting to be specified, taking into account the need for colour rendering.
4. Select luminaires that are efficient, having light distribution characteristics appropriate for the tasks and the environment, and not producing discomfort glare or serious veiling reflections.
5. Use the highest practical room surface reflectances, so as to achieve the best overall efficiency of the entire lighting system.
6. Integrate the lighting with the heating and air-conditioning systems, as dictated by climatic conditions, to save energy for cooling and heating purposes.
7. Provide a flexible lighting system, so that sections can be turned off or the lighting reduced when not needed.
8. Coordinate , when appropriate and when space permits, daylighting with electric lighting, ensuring that this does not introduce glare or other brightness imbalance in the environment.
9. Establish an adequate maintenance programme for periodic cleaning of the luminaires and room surfaces and for lamp replacement.[1]

These guidelines specifically exclude mention of the aesthetic requirements of the project, and it must be up to the architect and his lighting designer to ensure that in satisfying the guidelines, this is not at the expense of the lit appearance planned for the space.

---

[1]CIE. The Commission International de L'Eclarage

5 Calculations

Early methods of calculation ... model studies ... computer analysis ... artificial lighting ... examples of daylight studies

The very real importance of the daylighting strategy in modern buildings makes it a major consideration in design, and whilst an architect's innate understanding of the rules which have applied in the case of buildings since mediaeval times, the complications of modern structures and their interrelationships makes an understanding of daylighting desirable, if not essential. However it has to be said – and this is the experience gained from many of the case studies at the back of this book – the resulting daylighting strategy has evolved as much from the architect's past experience as from any detailed analysis and calculation.

Early daylight studies were limited to assessing the daylight penetration in sidelit rooms where a simple rule of thumb method was often used; since it was known that the head height of the window in a room influenced the depth to which the light would penetrate, a start could be made in determining the quantity of daylight where the light penetration was twice the head height of the window. An example of this might be in a stately home with windows reaching a ceiling height close to 7 m, the useful daylight would penetrate some 14 m into the space, and this is indeed our experience of such buildings. Likewise in a modern building with a much lower ceiling height of 2.5 m, the useful daylight penetration might be as little as 5 m or in a room with windows on both sides, a penetration of 10 m.

This is not to say that the quantity of daylight available at a distance of 5 m from a single window wall would provide a daylight factor considered adequate for office work overall, but it might be enough to provide a 5 per cent daylight factor close to the window with a 2 per cent daylight factor at the rear of the space, providing an overall sense of the space being daylit; and this would permit significant savings of energy if a system of 'daylight linking' artificial light was to be incorporated.

This simple rule of thumb, has to be hedged about with a large number of questions; such as the percentage of glazed area the window represents to the wall, the nature of the glazing, what external obstructions diminish the view of the sky outside the window and so on.

A useful start for an architect is provided by the publication *Good Practice Guide No. 245*, Desktop guide to Daylighting for Architects produced for the DETR by Professor Peter Tregenza in their Best Practice Programme on energy efficiency. This goes through a number of 'rules of thumb' and relates daylighting design to the different stages of the RIBA plan of work. Architects can learn a lot from the commonsense approach adopted in this little book, in establishing their initial design proposals before checking these out with the methods of computation available.

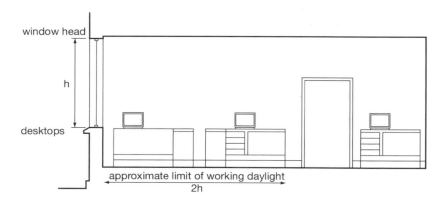

Rule of thumb. Daylight penetration

Buro Happold

The type and configuration of the window or windows, the nature of the glazing and their surroundings will make a significant difference, and whether the window is obscured by surrounding buildings, and how much of the floor area has an unobscured view of the sky. All these and other considerations need to be taken into account if an accurate calculation of the overall daylight picture is to be made.

From the architect's point of view, the physical modelling of a space has advantages. Simple design models are a part of his design tools, and have the advantage that they can be modified easily to accept changes to the section and layout. Alterations to the interior reflectances can be made and the interior effect photographed to show a client. Placing the model below an artificial sky and using a grid of photocells; such models at scales of 1/20 to 1/50 can be used to calculate the average daylight factor, and if found to be unsatisfactory the model can be modified to make the necessary changes to comply with the daylighting strategy, as depicted by the brief. A simple alternative which may be used as a rough check, is to place the model under an area of unobstructed sky.

It is not intended to go into the detail of the methods of calculation which are available; architects' offices will no doubt have the required computer software to deal with the straightforward problems of the calculation of the average daylight factor (DF) for buildings with traditional side windows. It is most important to establish the correct daylight strategy for a building in its environment, its orientation, and its neigbouring buildings, together with a 'client brief' that recognizes the advantages of the natural source.

The calculations for daylighting in large commercial buildings is intimately bound up with the requirements of artificial lighting, and by the means adopted for 'daylight linking'. When calculating the levels of daylight (DF) available during the day, this influences the level of the artificial light which must be available, since considerable savings of energy can be made by the sophisticated control systems now available.

Rather than duplicating the information on the methods of calculation which are available elsewhere, there follows a design report which considers both the daylighting and the artificial lighting of a modern office building, to indicate both methods of computer calculation and physical modelling.

EXAMPLE I

The report which follows is a report on the daylight and artificial lighting of offices for Wessex Water Operations centre in Bath for which the architects were Bennetts Associates. The report is included by the courtesy of Buro Happold, who were the structural, civil and building services engineers for the building.

NATURAL LIGHTING

The primary goal of the following daylight analysis is the evaluation of the potential of the design to provide appropriate levels of natural illumination.

Two methods of calculation are applied:

Method 1. Artificial sky
Method 2. Computer modelling

Method I.   Artificial sky

The artificial sky at Bath University School of Architecture was utilized to carry out a number of daylight tests on building sections. The artificial sky at the university conforms to the standard CIE overcast sky scaled to produce a variable 10,000 lux sky at model roof level. The tests were

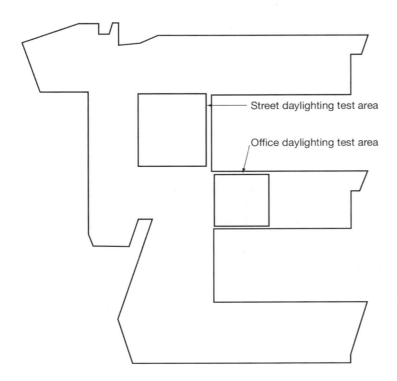

Street daylighting test area

Office daylighting test area

Plan of building indicating two areas for analysis
1. Street daylighting test area
2. Office daylighting test area

Buro Happold

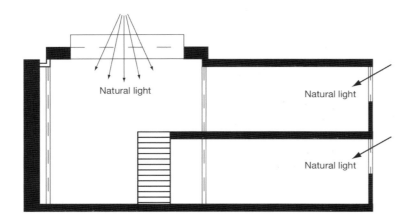

Sections of the three roof options for the street

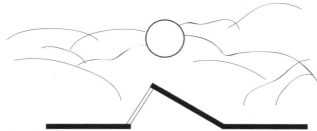

Translucent north light
and 100 percent blank on the
south side.
Frosted internal fins.

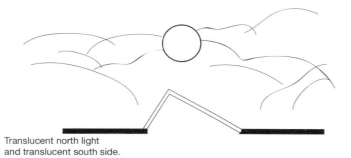

Translucent north light
and translucent south side.
Frosted internal fins.

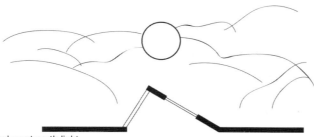

Translucent north light
and 50 percent translucent on the
south side.
Frosted internal fins.

Buro Happold

carried out to establish the daylight effects on a number of building forms and roof configurations.

CIBSE Guidelines recommend an average daylight factor of 5 per cent and a minimum of 2.5 per cent within general office areas with manual computer usage. Entrance areas and reception have a lower CIBSE recommendation of 2 per cent average and 0.6 per cent minimum. An improved level is anticipated due to the use of the entrance hall as a natural light well for the rear of the offices adjacent to the entrance hall.

Three options for the street were selected from a number which were considered, and a full daylight study was considered for each option.

Of these three, Option 1 was considered to be the most appropriate for the following reasons:

- Greater uniformity of lighting levels
- Reduction of glare into offices adjacent to the street
- The other two options tended to lead to 'overlighting' of the space
- Excessive solar gain into the street, creating overheating problems
- Excessive heat loss in summer.

Results from the model below the artificial sky:

Street Option 1, lower level

1. A minimum daylight factor of 3 per cent was measured with a maximum of 14 per cent for the lower office area; the average being 6 per cent.
2. The analysis indicated an average daylight factor of 7 per cent for the street at floor level, ensuring that a good daylight quality would be achieved.

Street Option 1, upper level

A minimum daylight factor of 4 per cent was measured for the upper office area with a maximum of 14 per cent at the perimeter, with an average of 7.4 per cent.

The model used for the analysis

Buro Happold

Conclusions

The results are very encouraging, and meet the requirements of the CIBSE Guidelines.

As expected the results for the upper level are slightly higher.

Whilst measurements were not taken directly up to the glazing line, it is expected that the figure would be higher at this point.

The comparison of the model at the street lower level with the subsequent computer results, shows acceptable agreement; 7 per cent average below the North lights and 4 to 12 per cent over the office place.

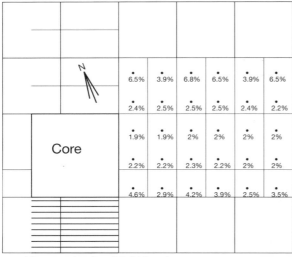

Measured natural light levels
typical office floor
upper level

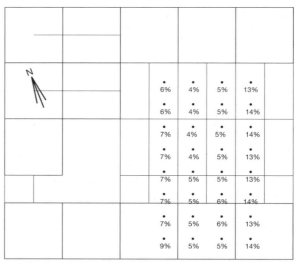

Option 1
Measured natural light levels
street north end
lower level

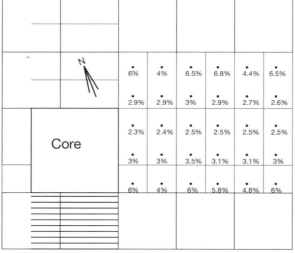

Measured natural light levels
typical office floor
lower level

Buro Happold

Option 1
Measured natural light levels
street north end
upper level

Buro Happold

Plans of the grid layouts for the upper and lower levels. Natural lighting contours measured by computer

Grid layouts for the position of photocell measurements with readings as follows: Street North End. Natural light levels. Lower and upper levels. Office Floor. Natural light levels. Lower and upper levels

Typical Office Wing results from the model, below the artifical sky:

Office Wing, lower level
A minimum daylight factor of 2.3 per cent was measured for the lower office area with a maximum of 6.8 per cent and average of 4 per cent.

Office Wing, upper level
A minimum daylight factor of 1.9 per cent was measured for the upper office, with a maximum of 6.8 per cent and average 3.2 per cent.

Conclusions

The minimum and average figures are slightly lower than the CIBSE recommendations, the prime reason being the shading elements. The model has solid south side shading elements at roof level, which is to be revised to an open louvred system to improve the conditions.

The effect of the shading system at roof level can be seen by examining the results between the lower and upper levels. The lower level shows a small improvement in the figures.

Wessex Water staff predominantly use PCs; as a result, the control of daylight is an important issue. Too much light would result in blinds being drawn.

Comparing the model studies with the computer results, the computer results are higher by the perimeter. This is to be expected as the computer readings cover the full floor plate, whilst the model studies are spot measurements only. The maximum computer level of 28 per cent is directly by the window. In addition, the measured model results have a built in reduction of 50 per cent to allow for the interior design, with fitted office space, furniture, colour schemes, changes to height, maintenance and light fittings.

Method 2.   Computer modelling

A computer study was undertaken to predict daylighting levels within the street and the central office wing.

The daylight studies assumed a CIE Standard overcast sky.

The daylight study of the open plan offices forming the central wing was undertaken with a daylight study of the street area indicated in the figure above.

In both cases the results were analysed at the working plane level.

The street lower level

The minimum daylight level was calculated to be 2.5 per cent.

The average daylight factor has been calculated to be 6.3 per cent. As with the central office area, this is a good value to achieve for a place predominantly lit by natural light.

The maximum daylight factor was found to be 22 per cent close to the windows.

Conclusions

The computer results compare well with the model studies

This is an important area of the building, where visitors gain a first impression of the building. The space should be well lit, welcoming, and feel natural in lighting terms.

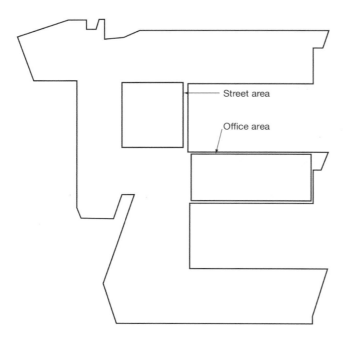

Street area

Office area

Natural lighting contours as measured by computer in the North Street and Lower office level, associated with location plan.

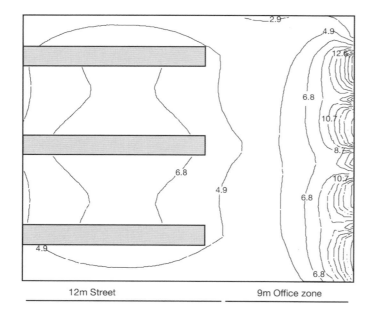

12m Street

9m Office zone

Natural lighting contours
north street and lower office level

Contours are shown as daylight percentages. The shaded zone over the street represent the north lights in the saw tooth roof.

Buro Happold

The Office Wing

The minimum daylight factor was calculated to be 1.78 per cent. This falls below the recommended levels, but only applies to 2 per cent of the floor area.

The average daylight factor was found to be 5.53 per cent. The recommended level of daylight in an office is between 2.5 per cent and 5 per cent. Bearing in mind that the daylight will be linked to the artificial lighting, the average level is adequate.

The maximum level of 28 per cent will cause problems of discomfort glare, but this occurs only in the immediate vicinity of the windows.

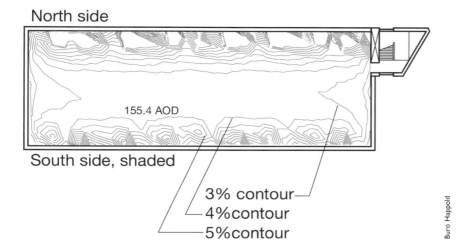

Natural lighting contours calculated by computer for a typical office floor

ARTIFICIAL LIGHTING

An analysis was carried out to consider the most energy efficient lighting system for the open plan spaces for Wessex Water New Operations Centre.

The design criteria is as follows:

- Lighting level 300–400 Lux
- Room height 3.2 m
- Window to window dimensions 15 m.

The design should take account of the following regulations which directly affect the lighting:

> The display screen equipment shall be free from disturbing glare and reflections
> There shall be an appropriate contrast between the screen and its background
> Adjustable coverings shall be provided for windows.

Several combinations of lamps and luminaires were investigated; the final recommendation was for the use of twin 35 w T5 luminaires, installed at a grid of 3 m by 2.4 m, suspended 400mm from the ceiling soffit.

To provide a design output of 400 lux, the system proposed provides 11.43 W/m.2 (for comparison the 'Good practice benchmark for offices would be 12 W/m. 2).

Luminaire choice

Lamp – Fluorescent

Reduced energy use, less than the conventional T8 lamp
Reduced glare with the use of three-dimensional glare control system
The T5 lamp uses less glass (40 per cent) and less mercury (80 per cent) than conventional lamps
Extended lamp life minimizes maintenance and reduces disposal and recycling costs

Luminaire body /louvre

Louvre high gloss mirror optic
Small lamp body size reduces materials of manufacture

Computer simulation of artificial lighting

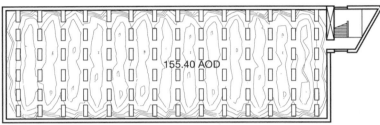

155.40 AOD

Energy consumption

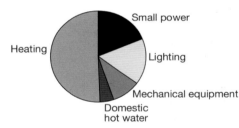

100 Kwh / m² / annum   Normalised building
8am - 5pm 5 days per week

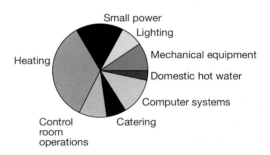

155 Kwh / m² / annum   Normalised hours plus
allowance
for computer
systems, catering and
24 hour control room operations

Delivered energy consumption (Kwh / m² / annum)

Buro Happold

Indirect/direct louvre with 25 per cent indirect and 75 per cent direct, this configuration produces high performance with high efficiency.

The artificial lighting was simulated by computer on the assumption that no natural lighting was available (a night time scenario) allowing for cleaning and lamp degradation. The results indicate a minimum light level of 235 Lux with a maximum of 919 Lux with an average of 636 Lux.

Conclusions

It can be concluded that the proposed artificial lighting solution will produce the correct lighting levels within the office spaces. At the design development stage an energy consumption figure of 100 Wh/m2/annum for normal working hours (excluding special energy requirements for computer suites control room and kitchen equipment).

There is no reason to amend this figure, but its success will depend upon the control regimes applied by the BEMS. This would no doubt take into account any savings of energy available due to daylight linking.

EXAMPLE 2

Whilst the first example is an extensive study, leading to a successsful conclusion in the subsequent built form, where model studies were compared with computer studies.

The following example is a preliminary study made at an early stage in the design of a building to check whether the daylight available would be satisfactory, or whether changes needed to be made to the daylight strategy.

DPA (Lighting Consultants) were commissioned to investigate the daylighting for a proposed extension to the Leeds College of Art and Design, Blenheim Walk Campus, providing new studio space over four floors. The building is referred to as the 'New Design and Communication Building'. The building designed by architects Aedas Architects Ltd contains large open-plan teaching studios, a studio/theatre

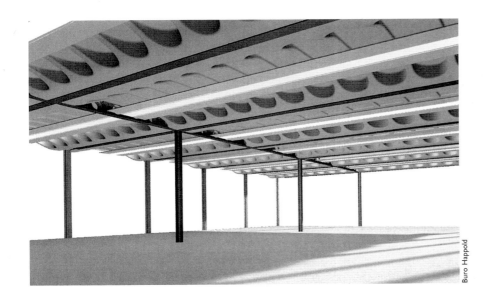

Computer simulation of a possible artificial lighting solution

Buro Happold

Photograph of an area in the completed building

Bennetts Associates Architects

photography area, and ancillary accommodation including WCs and offices.

The building layout is arranged around a central rectangular atrium area with one open-plan studio located either side of the atrium on the first and second floors. The lower ground and ground floor areas contain one open-plan studio per floor, each located on the northern side of the atrium. The atrium is to be provided with daylight via a large rooflight that spans the length of the atrium; daylight being allowed to penetrate downwards through the atrium to illuminate lower circulation areas, by means of voids located in the floor slabs above, at specific locations.

Walls provide valuable pin-up space in the open-plan studios, and as such a compromise was required between providing sufficient areas of glazing for adequate daylighting, whilst maintaining an acceptable amount of wall space for pinning-up.

In order to investigate the effect of increasing the glazed area to the wall abutting the atrium, measurements were undertaken with and without a solid wall inserted in the model.

The aim of the daylight study was to establish whether the level of daylight within the building would be adequate, based on the architects' initial proposals. The study was limited to the open-plan studio areas, a typical office area and the main atrium/circulation space.

The specific aims and objectives of the study included the following:

- Is the level of daylight to the open plan studios adequate?
- Is the level of daylight improved by increasing the amount of glazed area provided within the walls of the studio abutting the atrium area?
- Does the level of daylight achieved within these areas meet with current guidelines and/or legislation?

The approach adopted by the lighting designers was by means of direct measurement in a 1/50 model provided by the architects. The model had been accurately constructed in order to ensure the the window openings related closely to the proposed openings in the 'real' building. It was also important that the internal finishes within the model matched where possible the proposed surface finishes, with regard to the reflection factor, which have a significant effect on the lit environment.

The model was placed under the artificial sky at the Bartlett School of Architecture, which was hired for the study, so that daylight factor measurements might be obtained. The artificial sky consists of a hemispherical array of compact fluorescent luminaires, which can be individually programmed and controlled to provide a luminance distribution which matches that of the CIE overcast sky. Measurements of illuminance at specified locations can be provided by individual sensors or cells positioned within the model, compared with a reference cell located externally to the model allowing daylight factors (DF) to be calculated.

The scale model was placed in the artificial sky, and measurements of illuminance were taken at appropriate locations in each of the spaces under consideration, which, when compared to the reference cell, allowed the daylight factor at each grid point to be calculated.

From these measurements an average daylight factor for each group of measurements was calculated as the arithmetic mean of the individual daylight factor readings for each test session.

In the case of the open-plan studios measurements were taken with and without the solid wall abutting the atrium area. By conducting two

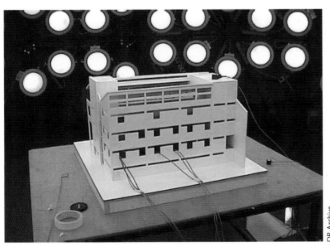
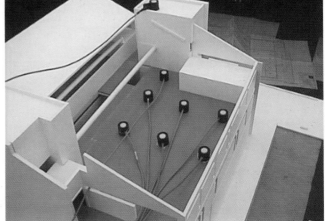

Photographs of the physical 1/50th scale model

comparative measurements, an assessment could be made of increasing the proportion of glazing within this wall.

(*Note*. Despite the accuracy of the model already described, the size of window openings used in the model did not exactly match those proposed for the building, as window mullions and other framing elements had been omitted for simplicity of construction. Depreciation factors were therefore applied to the measurements of the calculated daylight factors in order to produce more realistic values. These depreciation factors were based on an estimate of the relative areas of the mullions etc. The incorporation of realistic glazing is also difficult within a model and as such glazing is normally excluded; additional depreciation factors based on the light transmission values of the proposed glazing elements, are used to compensate for the reduced light transmission. Other depreciation factors are used to allow for dirt on the glass, the value of the factor depending upon the location of the building and the proposed maintenance regime. CIBSE provided appropriate values for these depreciation factors, based on experimental studies.)

Once the daylight factor measurements had been corrected for depreciation, the results were analysed and the average daylight factors compared with the relevant guidelines.

Finally the artificial sky simulator at the Bartlett is provided with an artificial sun that can be used for solar analysis, and this was used to provide for some images of the solar penetration into the building when subjected to sunny conditions at three-hour intervals for three periods of the year ... summer, winter solstice, and spring equinox, when the sun reaches its highest, lowest, and mid elevations respectively.

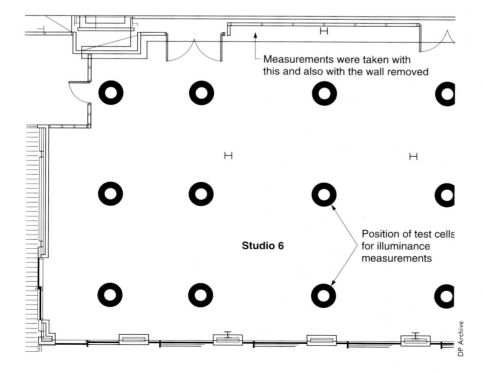

Sketch of the grid layout of the individual test cells for a second-floor studio

Measurements were taken with this and also with the wall removed

Studio 6

Position of test cells for illuminance measurements

DP Archive

The artificial sun uses a lamp in a parabolic reflector to simulate the sun's parallel rays of light

DP Archive

CONCLUSIONS

1. The open-plan studios located at the top of the building were well daylit having average daylight factors of over 5 per cent, with good uniformity across the spaces.
2. The average daylight factors predicted for the studios located on the ground and first floor were significantly lower, with average daylight factors lower than relevant guidelines.
3. The disparity between average daylight factors achieved for rooms located on different floors was larger than desirable.
4. The removal of the solid wall adjacent to the atrium increased the average daylight factors within each of the applicable studios and improved uniformity of daylight across the spaces. The increase in average daylight factors resulting from this improvement was not sufficient to ameliorate the deficiencies indicated above.

The results led the architect to reconsider the size and layout of the external glazing to specific areas of the building in order to increase the daylight levels within the ground and first floor studios. The addition of glazing to the partition wall was considered in order to increase the daylight penetration to the rear of the studios; increasing the amount of glazing within these walls would also improve the visual connection between the working areas of the building and adjacent circulation spaces. This was an important consideration in the lighting for working areas.

In conclusion, it is not suggested that methods of calculation or computer simulation are not relevant, but the more complicated the building, the more difficult, time consuming and expensive will they become, to a point where the study of simple models either in the exterior atmosphere or below an artificial sky, taken with their other advantages of simple modification to take into account necessary change and visual inspection, make them a worthwhile consideration.

Part II

6 Case Studies

INTRODUCTION

In *Lighting Modern Buildings*[1] the Case Studies were divided into eleven categories from Residential to Institutional/Public Buildings, as representing the different building functions. When discussing daylighting this categorization is less appropriate, since the criteria for daylighting art galleries have many of the same characteristics as the daylighting of supermarkets, despite the fact that the final solutions may be very different. A decision has been made not to repeat any of the Case Studies from the former book, but it may be of interest as an aide memoire to mention one or two in the area of the new categories.

The eight new categories used are as follows:

- Offices — To include public buildings and institutions
- Residential — To includes homes, hospitals and hotels
- Education — To include schools and university buildings
- Ecclesiastical — To include churches and chapels
- Leisure — To include leisure centres, sports halls and restaurants
- Display — To include art galleries and shops
- •Transport — To include over- and underground buildings
- Industrial — To include any form of industrial use.

A brief introduction to these categories is included, with illustrations of one or two of the original projects, where daylighting was critical.

Offices

Six offices were included in *Lighting Modern Buildings*, the most techically advanced in terms of daylighting being the solar office by Studio E in Doxford, where photovoltaic panels are employed to harness energy. The BA offices at Waterside are also an excellent example of daylighting in offices for a corporate headquarters.

Offices are one of the programmes where the requirements of vision are critical, and therefore the daylighting design must meet stringent requirements in terms of illumination level, and glare control; but where the intangibles are also of importance, such as the view out. In the

---

[1] *Lighting Modern Buildings*. Architectural Press, published 2000

Solar Office, Doxford

BA Headquarters

following examples it will be seen that the nature of the window design becomes crucial, with high tech designs being developed in buildings such as Hopkin's "Portcullis House" where the ventilation system is linked with the needs of acoustics, and daylighting to achieve a holistic solution.

Residential

The daylighting of residences is perhaps the least difficult problem for architects, but it becomes more of a problem interpreted by an hotel. Some of the finest examples of daylighting of homes was during the modern movement when the new solutions to structural problems allowed large areas of glazing.

Connell Ward and Lucas House, Moor Park

DP Archive

Education

It is in the field of educational buildings that some of the most innovative daylight solutions have been developed because the education authorities are insistant that in any new buildings for schools and universities the question of energy savings is fully investigated and solutions adopted.

Cranfield College Library

DP Archive

Ecclesiastical

The daylighting of churches has usually been dealt with in a satisfactory manner, because of the economic imperative. A church is not occupied for many hours in the day, but is visited more often. Therefore the daylighting must be sufficient for general use, perhaps backed up by additional artificial lighting when the church is in use.

An exception to this is the Methodist Church in Wisconsin, where a high tech solution has been adopted to overcome the difficulties associated with the climate, and the site, leading to an economic solution, well related to its location within a hillside (Case Study, pp 142–143).

Bagsvaerd Church, Denmark

David Loe

Leisure

This is a further example where it is recognized that daylighting is best and many examples could be found of swimming pools, leisure centres and sports halls relying entirely on daylighting during the day, provided that associated problems of solar glare can be overcome.

A particularly interesting example of Sports Lighting is in the Chelsea Club, where the natural advantages of the "view out" have been eliminated. The use of a special wall panelling permits daylight to enter, but which restricts the view in to allow for the paramount need in this instance for privacy, in contrast to a further example of leisure lighting in which daylight has totally replaced the need for artificial light.

Inland Revenue, Nottingham

DP Archive

Display

This category was incorporated in the previous book by Shops/Display and Art Galleries, but is now amalgamated into a single category, since, while the functions of a project may differ widely, the criteria demanded are not dissimilar.

There may be little similarity between the interior of the Sainsbury Supermarket in Greenwich, and the lighting of the Charioteer statue in Delphi; but the object, that of emphasis on the one hand, of the goods on display, and on the other, the folds in the stone statue's garments, are both derived successfully from overhead daylighting. The difference in the case of Sainsbury, being the additional artificial lighting to highlight the gondolas with their display of goods for sale.

Transport

Whilst above ground transport buildings were generally designed for the economic use of daylight, with airports and railway stations leading the field, the concepts had rarely been applied to underground stations, so this is an area ripe for development.

The Jubilee Line stations are a good example, where daylighting has been considered an important part of the brief, carrying on the tradition of good design of the original underground stations, but with the addition of daylight (Case Study, pp 180–187).

The Burrell Collection, Glasgow

The King Khalid Airport, Riyadh, Saudi Arabia

Industrial

Some industrial installations require high levels of lighting for manufacture and assembly which cannot be provided by daylight alone; however daylight can be used successfully to provide the overall environmental light, whilst artificial light can supplement this where required. Many factories were built for various reasons in the twentieth century to exclude the natural source.

York Shipley Factory, Basildon

Arup

There is little that resembles "the dark satanic mills" of the 19th Century in our latest factory designs, and a fine example of this is the Cummins Engine Company Factory built near Manston Airport in Kent (Case Study, pp 190–191). Lit by lines of overhead daylighting, it also provides side lighting from large windows, which add a light and airy appearance to the interior. Such buildings do have to rely on artificial lighting for the dull days, and ideally these should have daylight linking, to ensure that the electric light is used only when required.

Selected List of Case Studies

OFFICES

Reichstag Renovation	Foster
Provincial Capitol, Toulouse	Venturi Scott-Brown
88 Wood Street	Richard Rogers
Portcullis House	Michael Hopkins
77 Wicklow Street	Squire & Partners
Arup Campus	Arups
MOD, Abbeywood	Sir Percy Thomas
Host Street, Bristol	Jeremy Johnson-Marshall

RESIDENTIAL

Great Eastern Hotel	Manser Associates
De Syllas House	Avanti Architects

EDUCATION

Worlds End School, Enfield	Architect's Co-Partnership
Orchard Learning and Resource Centre	Ahrends Burton and Koralek
University of Warwick, Union	Casson Conder Partnership
City Learning Centre, Bristol	Alec French Partners
New Faculty of Education, UWE	Alec French Partners
Polk County Science Centre	John McAslan and Partners
Goldsmiths College	Allies and Morrison
Michael Young Building, OU	Jestico+Whiles
Riverhead School, Sevenoaks	ADP Architects

ECCLESIASTICAL

Central United Methodist Church	William Wenzler and Associates
Rothco Chapel	Philip Johnson, Barnstone and Aubry

LEISURE

Chipping Norton Leisure Centre	Feilden Clegg Bradley
Chelsea Club	Fletcher Priest
Serpentine Gallery Pavilion	Toyo Ito
American Community School	Studio E

DISPLAY

New rooms at Royal Academy	R. Smidt
Sainsbury, Greenwich	Chetwood Associates
Museum of Country Life, Ireland	Office of Public Works, Dublin
Delphi Museum, The Charioteer	AN Tombazis and Associates
Hong Kong, Lei Yue Mun	ASL Dangerfield

TRANSPORT

Jubilee Line Underground	
Southwark	McCormac Jamieson Prichard
Canada Water	Ron Herron/Imagination
Canary Wharf Tube	Foster and Partners
Stratford Station	Wilkinson Eyre

INDUSTRIAL

Cummins Engine Company	Bennetts Associates
Gridshell Building, Weald and Downland	Edward Cullinan Associates

OFFICES

The Reichstag, Berlin

Architect	Foster and Partners
Lighting Design	Claude Engle
Client	Federal Republic of Germany

The reconstruction of the old Berlin Reichstag Building from its mutilated condition after the Second World War, to its brilliant new form was rooted in four main principles:

- The Bundestag's significance as a democratic forum
- A commitment to public accessibility
- A sensitivity to history
- A rigorous environmental agenda.

The architects have addressed each of these principles, but the purpose of this Case Study is to concentrate on the last of these objectives, in which daylighting is clearly a priority.

The brief for an energy efficient building was developed by the design team in conjunction with the Federal Government, with low fossil fuel and CO_2 emissions leading to a more sustainable architecture. This led to the following solutions:

1. Combined heat and power generation, associated with seasonal energy storage.
2. The use of biomass (rape seed oil) as a renewable energy source for the production of electricity, the result of which is a 94 per cent reduction in carbon dioxide emissions.
3. Natural ventilation and natural daylight.
4. Solar energy. The use of 100 solar panels on the roof, providing a peak output sufficient to drive the exhaust air ventilation system of the main plenary chamber, together with other shading devices within the dome.

One of the key aims has been to optimize the use of natural daylight throughout the building, to minimize the use of artificial lighting, thus reducing electricity consumption.

The main feature of the building, as experienced by the general public is the cupola or dome on the roof, located above the plenary chamber, The cupola is crucial to the daylighting and ventilation strategies for the building. At its core is the light sculptor which rises from the top of the chamber, opening out towards the cupola. This reflective cone provides the solution to lighting and ventilating the chamber. The reflector is a concave faceted cone, covered with a battery of 360 angled mirrors which together form a giant fresnel lens working like a lighthouse in reverse, directing horizontal light down to the chamber. The

cone is associated with a moveable sun-shield blocking solar gain and glare during the day, whilst at night the process is reversed, with the cupola becoming a beacon to establish the location and purpose of the building as a symbolic and vital part of the Federal Capital.

The only way truly to appreciate the science and artistry of the building is to experience the magic of the daylighting effects, by visiting it. The goal of the design team has been to create a building that will be energy efficient, wherever possible using natural renewable energy sources to provide maximum comfort, striving towards a more 'sustainable architecture'.

This light sculptor is a part of the ventilation system bringing air up towards the top of the dome whilst at the same time it reflects horizontal light to the chamber.

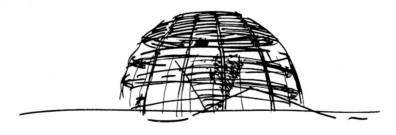

Norman Foster's initial concept for the dome, and the light sculptor

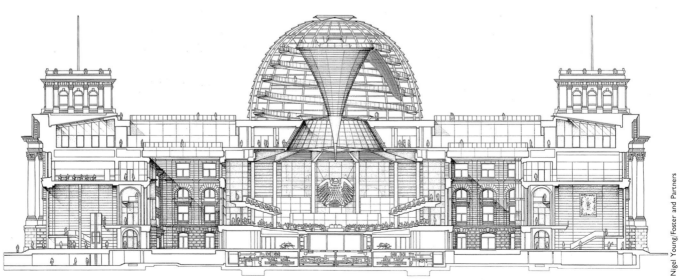

Section illustrating the relationship of the plenary chamber, with the dome and light sculptor

Nigel Young/Foster and Partners

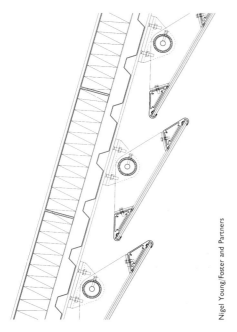

Detail of the 'angled mirrors' which reflect light down into the chamber

Nigel Young/Foster and Partners

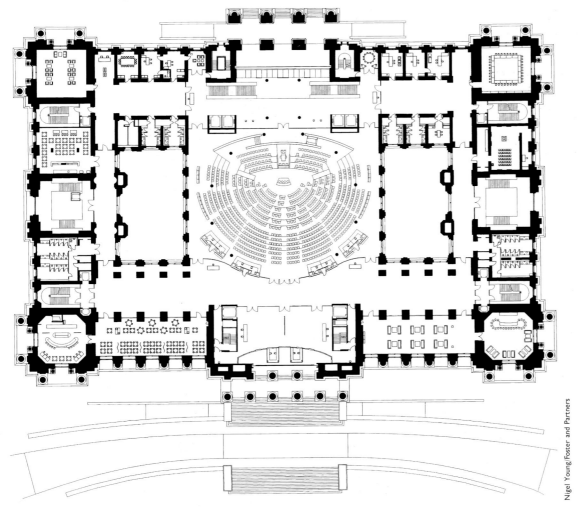

Nigel Young/Foster and Partners

Plan showing the central plenary chamber, with its relationship to the main entrance

Nigel Young/Foster and Partners

Light sculptor and the dome

Nigel Young/Foster and Partners

The plenary chamber and dome above

MP lobby, showing side window daylighting

Provincial Capitol Building, Toulouse, France

Architect	Venturi Scott Brown & Associates
Associate architects	Hermet-Blanc-Lagausie-Momens-Atelier A4 and Anderson/Swartz Architects
Lighting design	Cabinet Berthon
Client	Conseil General de la Haute-Garonne, Toulouse, France

The capitol building in Toulouse was won in architectural competition, and consists of an administrative and legislative complex to include offices, the assembly chamber, public services and support spaces, with three levels of underground parking. The design challenge for the architects was to introduce this inherently large building complex into a small-scale residential and commercial area of Toulouse, a challenge fully met by the design.

What is important in the context of this book however, is in the nature and solution to the daylighting, and no more so than in the assembly chamber. For whilst the layout and design of the administative offices allows them to be lit by conventional windows, the solution to the lighting of the assembly chamber called for an entirely different approach.

It was important that the interior of the hall should appear to be a legislative chamber, not an amphitheatre; and for this reason the hall should give the impression of being daylit, even if for reasons dictated by the use of electronic projection, the hall needed on occasions to be darkened.

The solution adopted is to allow controlled daylight to enter from clerestory windows around the top of the space, whilst the impression of daylight is gained from a series of false windows at a lower level. The clerestorey windows allow the view of real clouds during the day and introduce daylight into the hall, controlled when needed by movable sun screens. The false windows give the impression of lightness, which is desirable for meetings held during the day, and can continue during the evening, but is controllable when needed for the electronic projection.

Behind the the false windows are gently lit acoustical walls with murals depicting Margritte-like clouds. The impression received by the combination of real and simulated daylight was modelled at the design stage by computer modelling,

The architects have described their daylight strategy as 'more intuitive' than by means of quantative analysis, but nevertheless, a good deal of schematic design was undertaken to investigate the possible advantages of *brise*

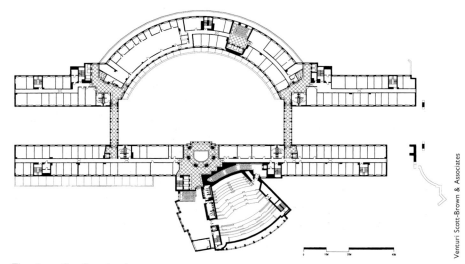

The plan at first floor level

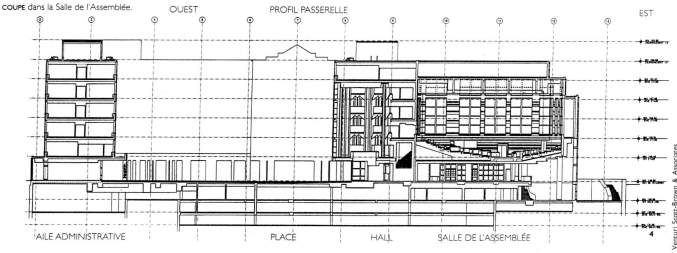

COUPE dans la Salle de l'Assemblée.   OUEST   PROFIL·PASSERELLE   EST

AILE ADMINISTRATIVE   PLACE   HALL   SALLE DE L'ASSEMBLÉE

The section

Interior of hall

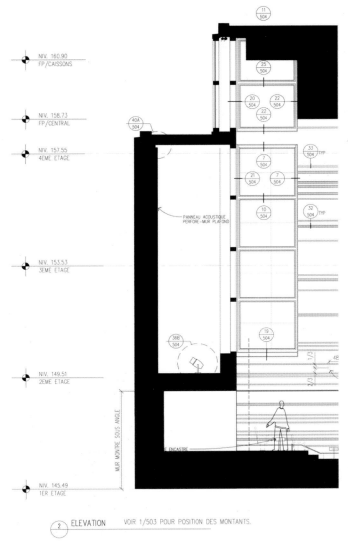

Venturi Scott-Brown & Associates

② ELEVATION VOIR 1/503 POUR POSITION DES MONTANTS.

Detail through false windows

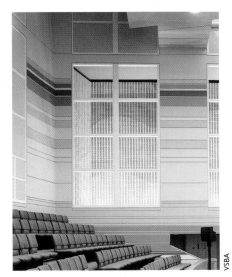

Acoustical 'cloud' wall. (See also the third plan above)

soleil and other forms of sun control, before deciding on the nature of the clerestoreys. Winter and summer solstice diagrams were studied to maximize window size, whilst minimizing the harmful impact of direct daylight and sunlight from the clerestorys. Highly efficient glazing was specified to satisfy the clients' concerns about heat gain, whilst solar shades were added to eliminate glare.

Landscape view of the meeting room

Matt Wargo for VSBA

88 Wood Street

Architect	Richard Rogers Partnership
Structural and Service Engineers	Ove Arup and Partners
Client	Daiwa. Europe Properties PLC

Completed in 1999, the offices at 88 Wood Street, in the heart of the city of London, is the first major office block built by the Richard Rogers Partnership since Lloyds of London was completed in 1986. Won in competition in 1990, the original brief was to create a prestige headquarters for the Daiwa Banking Corporation, but the original concept design was hit by the recession in both Japan and London, and a new brief in 1994 called for a speculative office block.

The building is more than a third larger than the original concept, rising in three linked steps of 10, 14 and 18 storeys, comprising 22,600 m² of dealing and administrative facilities. 88 Wood Street addresses the demands of the office market

with great elegance; it it is a building of unusual transparency.

It is this transparency which declares its daylighting credentials; for the intention was to provide an office building which would maximize the use of daylight and give the impression of being wholly lit by natural light. The floor plates are arranged so that no-one sits more than 13 m from a window, and that artificial lighting is not generally required during the day.

The windows are triple glazed on all but the north side, with internal blinds which are operated automatically to control solar glare.

The building's 'active' façade comprises the world's largest double glazed units, measuring 3 m by 4 m. The inner faces of the external

panes have a low E (emissivity) coating, which further reduces internal solar gain. In addition a third glass panel is provided to the 'climate' façade. A 140 mm cavity between the third panel and the double glazed units is provided with integral horizontal venetian blinds with perforated slats. Photo cells on the roof monitor the external light conditions adjusting the angles of the blinds, thus minimizing sun glare and heat gain.

The artificial lighting is 'daylight linked' with the exterior light levels, to reduce the energy required during the day; but because the building is a speculative office block, the individual tenants have a degree of control of the artificial lighting system adopted for their own areas. As one would expect, the different tenants have developed their own areas in terms of their own individual needs and tastes; but the building design is robust enough to cope with these idiosyncrasies and a walk around the building indicates an overall sense of quality, incorporating the latest advances in technology and energy conservation, and offers uninterrupted views over the city.

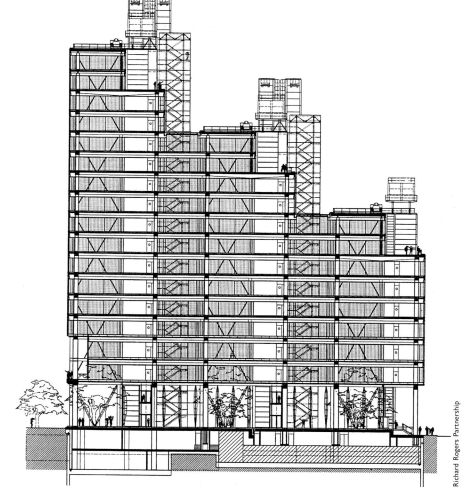

Richard Rogers Partnership

Building elevation, this shows a regular and unimpeded office space across an irregular site

Office floor plan at Level 8

Richard Rogers Partnership

Plan at street level

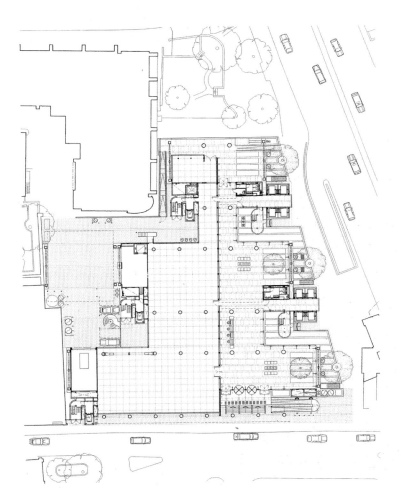

Richard Rogers Partnership

Main elevation

Katsuhisa Kida

Katsuhisa Kida

Unoccupied floor space

Katsuhisa Kida

View to foyer from Level 1 Walkway

Typical occupied floor

Detail of window with opening leaf

View out over London from an office

Portcullis House, Westminster

Architect	Michael Hopkins and Partners
Engineer	Ove Arup & Partners
Client	House of Commons, Palace of Westminster

The history of the site for the new Parliamentary Building – or as it is now called, Portcullis House – goes back several decades; the architect Michael Hopkins's involvement started in 1989 with a space audit of the accommodation which might be required for Members of Parliament. It was not until the interchange for the new Jubilee Line extension at Westminster Underground was approved, that this paved the way for a radical new approach to the site; in which the new Parliamentary Building was conceived as an integral planning and structural solution together with a much enlarged underground station.

Located in a world heritage site, placed between Pugin's Houses of Parliament and Norman Shaw's Scotland Yard, the site posed many problems which required a unique solution to provide 210 individual offices for Members of Parliament, with all the associated ancillary accommodation; together with a pedestrian connection under Bridge Street to 'the House' to enable Members of Parliament to react swiftly to the division bell.

The daylighting strategy is determined by the plan, in which the MPs' offices are arranged around a hollow rectangular courtyard, with rooms on four floors for the MPs, which look outwards or inwards to the courtyard; rooms have balconies and french windows with rooms to the outside having their own bay window.

The public face of the building at street level presents a colonnade to Bridge Street, containing shops and the entrance to the Tube. The main entrance to the building itself is from the river side, on the Embankment. At ground level the courtyard has an enclosed area with a vaulted glazed roof, where MPs can congregate and meet their constituents. Two rows of trees create an avenue with a central water feature, all enlivened by excellent daylighting.

At the first floor level are housed meeting rooms and rooms for public select committees, whilst support facilities are housed at the lower ground level.

The building is not air conditioned, and the brief for the building required that the energy consumption should be only one third of that for a traditional air-conditioned building. The section through the window (see fourth plan) indicates the triple glazed window used for

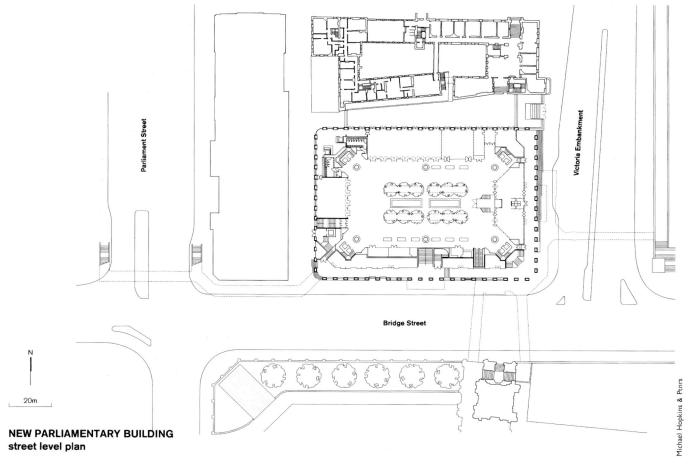

NEW PARLIAMENTARY BUILDING
street level plan

Street level plan. Shows central covered courtyard

Michael Hopkins & Ptnrs

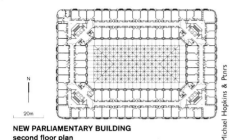

NEW PARLIAMENTARY BUILDING
second floor plan

Plan at 2nd-4th level showing the MPs' rooms

Michael Hopkins & Ptnrs

Plan of a pair of MPs' rooms with intermediate staff

Michael Hopkins & Ptnrs

the Members' rooms. The windows, together with the internal blind system, were modelled as part of an EU Joule II study together with the suggested system of ventilation in a mock-up in Southern Italy in accelerated tests to prove the method of daylighting and ventilation.

The window detail shows a projecting light shelf which bounces natural light on to the white concrete arched ceiling into the interior of the room, and although research suggests that this does not increase the 'level' of daylight in a space, it assists its distribution, whilst at the same time acting as solar shading.

Clerestoreys above the bookcases at the rear of the room allow daylight to escape from the interior of the Members' rooms to enliven the internal corridor beyond what would otherwise be a totally artificially lit space.

Key

1 Patinated bronze facade: bay window
2 Lightshelf: daylight reflector and solarshade
3 Lightshelf: artificial lighting
4 Gullwing precast structural slab
5 Facade clerestorey cavity and extract plenum
6 Retractable blind within window cavity
7 English oak panel
8 Leather bench seat
9 Precast concrete partition

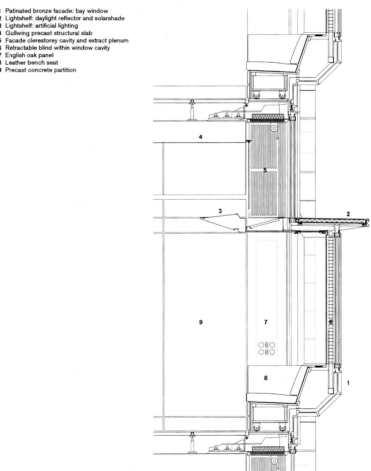

500mm

PORTCULLIS HOUSE
WINDOW DETAIL

Section through a typical window to a Member's room

Michael Hopkins & Ptnrs

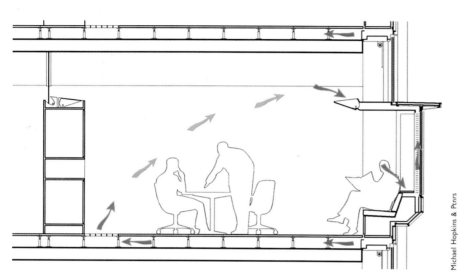

Energy section. Ventilation to MPs' room

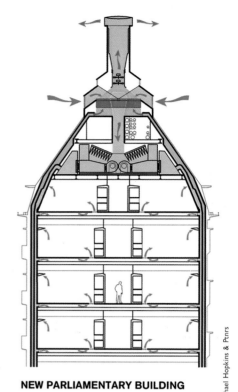

**NEW PARLIAMENTARY BUILDING
energy section**

Diagram relating the daylighting to the
system of ventilation

Michael Hopkins & Ptnrs

Michael Hopkins & Ptnrs

Exterior of the building, to show the colonnading to Bridge Street

DP Archive

The interior courtyard with glazed roof

Richard Davis

Richard Davis

Members' room, looking towards the window

Richard Davis

Members' room looking to rear with clerestorey

Richard Davis

Corridor at first floor level overlooking the courtyard

Squire's Offices, 77 Wicklow Street

Architect and lighting design   Squire and Partners, Architects
Client   Squire and Partners

The architectural practice of Squire and Partners has converted the ground and basement floors of a 1930s industrial warehouse into offices for their architectural practice.

It is clear that the daylighting strategy has been influential in the creation of what is a most successful conversion. The lower ground floor originally had no natural light; so the ground floor slab was cut back 6 m either side, with full height glazing at street level, allowing daylight to permeate both of the open plan floors. Clearly the daylight factors in the central areas at each level will not provide sufficient light for the office, which is lit by artificial sources, but it gives that all-important daylight 'feel' with views to the outside far from the side windows.

The photographs indicate the quality of the spaces provided, which include the entrance hall, general architects' office space, committee rooms, cafeteria, and storage areas.

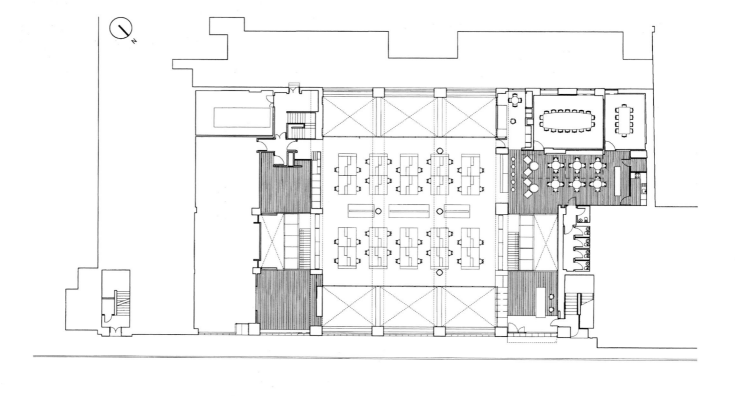

Ground floor plan

Squire & Partners

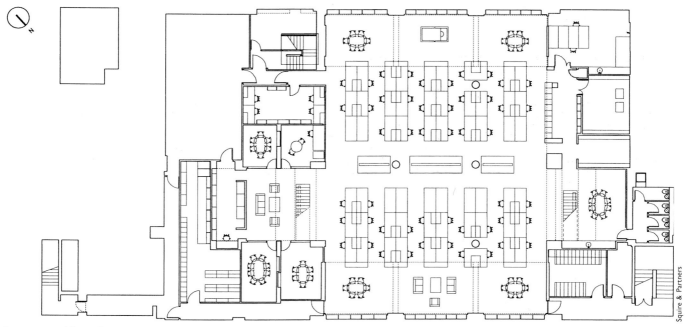

Lower ground floor plan

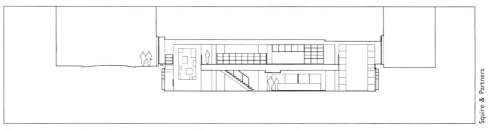

Cross section, to show the cut-away ground floor

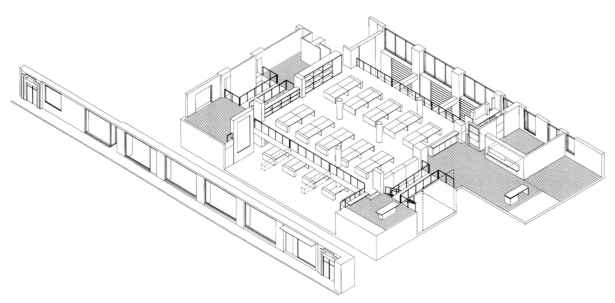

Axonometric of the overall layout

Exterior of the 1930s building

Lower ground to show the set back ground floor, close to the roadside

Central area of office with views towards the roadside

DP Archive

The cafeteria

DP Archive

Arup Campus, Solihull

Architect & Engineer	Arup Associates
Client	Arup

It is not surprising that when the architects – Arup Associates, the lighting designers – Arup Lighting, get together with the engineers – Ove Arup and Partners, that the resulting offices built in Solihull for themselves should be state of the art; where the daylighting is linked with the artificial lighting, which together with the passive structure, has led to a comfortable low energy and sustainable architecture.

The building has a general north-west, south-east orientation, an orientation designed to optimize the natural lighting whilst respecting the site's constraints and optimizing use of the available space. Looking at the exterior of the building, it is not surprising that it is known affectionately by the locals as the 'chicken shed' due to the projecting roof pods placed at intervals along the roof line.

These pods are the key to the success of the natural environment, incorporating skylights to ensure good levels of light penetration to the central areas of the offices; whilst at the same time incorporating louvres to enable stack effect ventilation, forming a part of the environmental control strategy for the building.

The building consists of two parallel pavilions of two storeys each, approximately 60 m long by 24 m deep, designed to minimize the number of levels in the building, with mezzanines and floor openings used to maximize internal staff communication, with good light penetration to the lower levels.

To ensure good control of glare, the glazing to the north-east and south-west façades is minimized, whilst the use of external solar shading to the southerly façades ensures that the solar heat gain is prevented from entering the building, enabling the strategy of natural ventilation to be effective. All of the main elevations incorporate shading devices to control solar gain, and where occupants are seated close to a window manually operated louvres allow personal control, to reduce local heat gain.

On the south-east double height façade, where users are not seated close to windows, electrically operated exterior blinds are controlled by the building management system with manual override. On the northern elevation manually operated interior blinds are available when needed, as the reduction in direct solar penetration is not as critical.

A sophisticated system of control is used for the artificial lighting, designed to incorporate both proximity control sensing, and daylight linking; in which combined sensors are integrated into the light fittings. The lighting units were specially developed for the campus, as a part of the overall lighting strategy.

The light fittings contain both indirect uplighting and direct downlighting; but it has been found in operation that the amount of the upward light can be reduced, as the level of natural light is more than sufficient, in which the spaces appear light and airy even on comparatively overcast days.

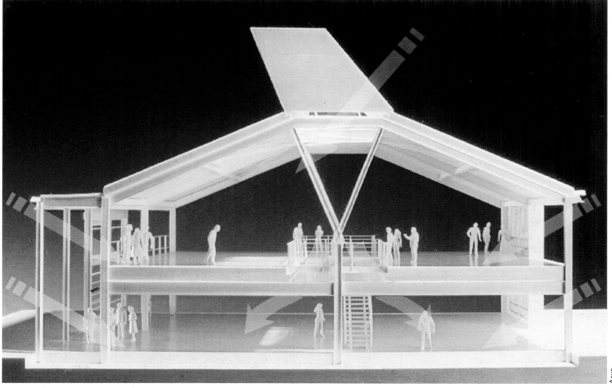

Section of model to illustrate the daylighting

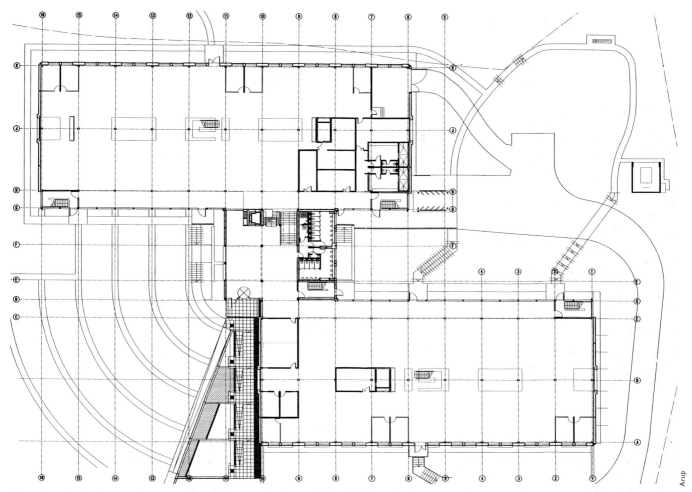

Plan at lower level, showing the two wings, and indicating the location of the daylight pods above

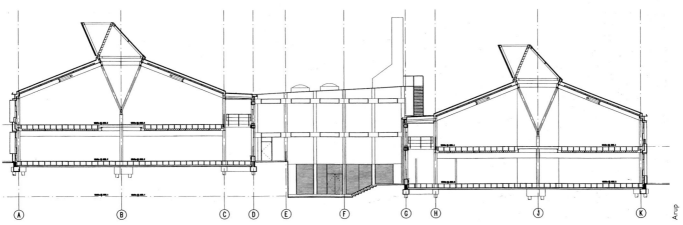

Section of the building

Elevation to show projecting pods

Arup

Exterior to show the application of reduced glazing and fixed louvres to southerly elevations

DP Archive

External hand-operated louvres to the south east elevation, for the occupants close to the windows

Interior of office illustrating the artificial lighting system related to a circulation aisle

MOD Abbey Wood campus

Architect	Percy Thomas Partnership (PTP)
Engineer	Hoare Lea
Client	Ministry of Defence, Defence Procurement Agency

The Defence Procurement Agency is responsible for purchasing equipment for the armed services, and was originally housed in sites widely dispersed throughout the country. In 1992 the MOD took possession of a 98-acre site near Bristol, with the aim of creating a totally self-sustaining office campus to house 5500 staff together with all the ancillary accommodation, to include car parking, technical library, storage, simultaneous interpretation, lecture and conference facilities, sports, training, catering and a 100 place crèche, resulting in a complex of 1.3 million sq.ft., one of the largest office developments in Europe.

The scheme design resulted from a cooperative effort between all the design disciplines, in which the following key elements were identified,

- Occupant performance
- Daylighting
- Views
- Ventilation
- VDT use throughout
- Energy consumption
- Life cycle costs

Although this list is not said to be in any order of priority, it is clear that the role to be played by daylighting, tied in as it is with energy, views, ventilation and occupant satisfaction was considered to be of first importance. With some 20,000 m^2 of office glazing it was necessary to ensure that the elemental window design was both energy efficient and cost effective, whilst satisfying the needs of the occupants.

The type of glazing to be used was thoroughly investigated, with ten systems modelled in full annual weather conditions.

The final choice rested on a system of triple glazing, with opening lights for ventilation, providing an approximate percentage glazing of 40 per cent of the external wall area. Solar control is by internal blinds incorporated in the triple glazing. The use of external *brise soleil* was outweighed by their capital, maintenance and replacement costs. It was shown that 'interplane' blinds were more desirable in achieving enhanced performance and a reduction in cleaning.

The type of glass used was 'clear,' designed to enhance the importance of the view out; which also reduced the contrast between open and closed windows; and whilst some of the high tech glasses, such as specialist coated or tinted glass, were investigated, it was felt that their long term viability had not been sufficiently established.

The section through a typical four-storey office block with its central street shows that no-one is more than 6.5 m away from a

Masterplan of the complex

window, and the impression within the offices is one of natural light.

The quantity of daylight available is automatically linked to the level of artificial lighting by the use of 'intelligent' light fittings, allowing considerable savings in electricity, and a consequent reduction in CO_2 production. Using 350 lux as a standard, it has been established that on average only 36 per cent of the artificial lighting is required during the day. The installed load is 16watts/m^2.

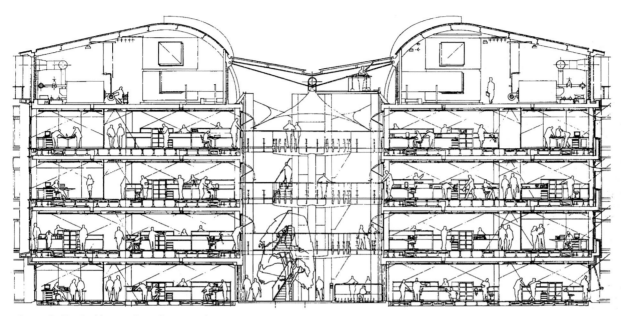

Section of typical office building to show the internal street

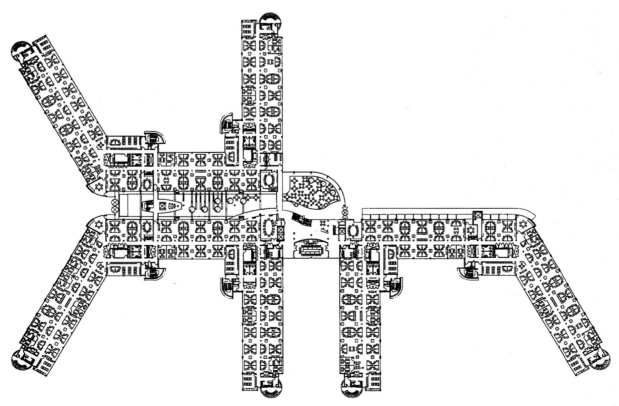

Plan of a typical neighbourhood

Internal street

Percy Thomas Partnership

Interior of daylit café

Percy Thomas Partnership

Exterior view to show the landscaping and its
relationship with the buildings

Percy Thomas Partnership

Window detail to show sun control

Percy Thomas Partnership

Host Street, Bristol

Architect and lighting design	Jeremy Johnson-Marshall
Client	Kinneir Dufort Design Ltd.

The majority of the Case Studies are examples of new buildings, where the daylighting strategy has been one of the important determinants of the design. In the case of Host Street, this was an existing nineteenth century listed industrial building, where 'new use' demanded additional floor space in the roof which had seen no daylight.

In the nineteenth century cane sugar had been processed on the plantations and sent to England as crude molasses, where it was refined. Host Street is a typical industrial building erected for this purpose, adjoining the docks in the centre of the city. It has cast iron columns supporting heavy timber floors, and had been converted into offices, studios

and prototyping workshops for a firm of industrial designers.

The top floor however was limited by a 1.7 m headroom below heavy roof truses, and to gain the extra space required it was decided to remove the existing roof and to raise it, allowing the addition of an extra floor. This created the opportunity, indeed the necessity, to consider the entry of natural light to the newly created floor areas.

The method adopted can be be seen in the accompanying plans and sections. The new roof matched the old at the front, but a glazed gable was included at the rear, allowing daylight to penetrate to the new floor areas. The proposals permitted better daylight to

the new areas than that available to those below. Due to the listed nature of the buildings, these dramatic changes were the subject of long discussions, but the final results have achieved a working commercial building retaining its open industrial spaces.

A series of photographs taken on completion of the project clearly illustrate the quality of the spaces, and the success of the daylighting strategy adopted. Without the careful consideration of the natural lighting adopted this project would have been untenable.

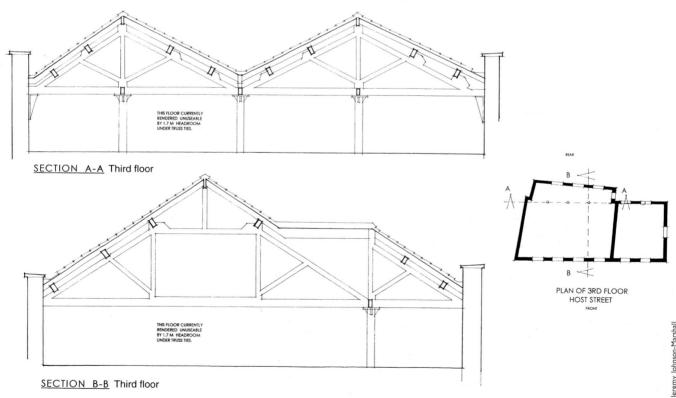

SECTION A-A Third floor

THIS FLOOR CURRENTLY RENDERED UNUSEABLE BY 1.7 M HEADROOM UNDER TRUSS TIES.

SECTION B-B Third floor

Original roof section. This shows the 1.7 m headroom

PLAN OF 3RD FLOOR
HOST STREET
FRONT

Jeremy Johnson-Marshall

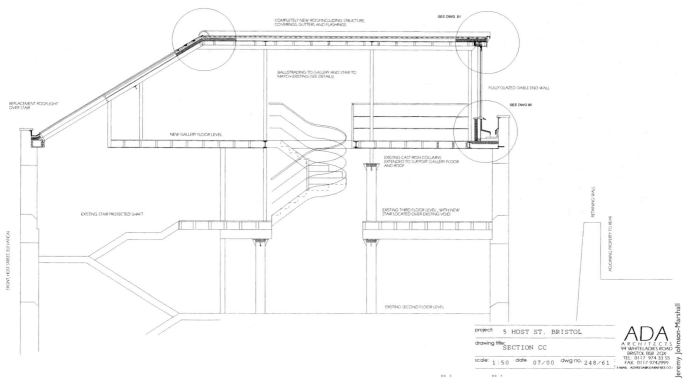

BUILDING REGULATIONS NOTES

SEE DETAIL DRAWINGS FOR CONSTRUCTION INFORMATION
SEE ENGINEERS INFORMATION FOR STRUCTURE
NB.
GALLERY FLOOR OVER STAIR AND WC AREA IS PART OF FIRE
PROTECTION TO STAIR. CONSTRUCTION IS CURRENTLY PROPOSED
AS LINOLEUM ON 22MM T&G CHIPBOARD ON 200X50 SW JOISTS
WITH 12MM PLASTERBOARD BELOW.

COMPLETELY NEW ROOF INCLUDING STRUCTURE, COVERINGS, GUTTERS AND FLASHINGS

SEE DWG 91

BALUSTRADING TO GALLERY AND STAIR TO MATCH EXISTING (SEE DETAILS)

FULLY GLAZED GABLE END WALL

REPLACEMENT ROOFLIGHT OVER STAIR

SEE DWG 90

NEW GALLERY FLOOR LEVEL

EXISTING CAST IRON COLUMNS EXTENDED TO SUPPORT GALLERY FLOOR AND ROOF

EXISTING STAIR PROTECTED SHAFT

EXISTING THIRD FLOOR LEVEL, WITH NEW STAIR LOCATED OVER EXISTING VOID

RETAINING WALL

FRONT, HOST STREET, ELEVATION

ADJOINING PROPERTY TO REAR

EXISTING SECOND FLOOR LEVEL

project: 5 HOST ST, BRISTOL
drawing title: SECTION CC
scale: 1:50   date 07/00   dwg no. 248/61

ADA
ARCHITECTS
94 WHITELADIES ROAD
BRISTOL BS8 2QX
TEL: 0117 974 33 55
FAX: 0117 9742999
E-MAIL ADYRES@LEARNFREE.CO

Jeremy Johnson-Marshall

New section showing the additional floor

DP Archive

The exterior of the building

Interior. View up the new staircase

Interior. View showing the new floor area

RESIDENTIAL

Great Eastern Hotel

Architect	The Manser Practice; Interiors: Conran
Lighting consultant	DPA Lighting Consultants/Maurice Brill
Client	Great Eastern Hotel

The Great Eastern Hotel has had a somewhat chequered history from its early promise as one of London's great railway hotels at the end of the nineteenth century, similar to those at St. Pancras, Paddington or Euston. Completed in 1884 and extended in 1899–1901, it had suffered serious dereliction and neglect.

Its close connection to Liverpool Street station had not served it well, with a carriageway to serve the station below severing the building and with railway platforms below forcing the kitchens to be located at the fourth floor level, it was far from being ideal.

The redevelopment of the hotel by the Manser Practice, with interiors by Conran is an extraordinary achievement, in which the hotel now has all the advantages of modern servicing together with the calm interiors of a bygone age. It is of interest that the Manser Practice was responsible for the first really modern hotel built in this country, at Heathrow Terminal 4 (see Case Study 32 in *Lighting Modern Buildings*) and that in this reconstruction project they have brought all the expertise of creating beautiful daylit spaces learnt from the new.

The success of the daylighting design can be boiled down to three main areas: the Lift Lobby and Atrium, the Main Dining room, and the Bedrooms .

The lift lobby and atrium
A 'borehole' of light, a circular lightwell, penetrates the ceiling of the entrance lobby, rising through the full height of the building. This entrance lobby leads to the main atrium formed by extending two existing light wells, which rise throughout the building, the glazed roof of which provides daylight to adjacent bedrooms in addition to funnelling light below.

A decision was made to acid etch the under-surface of the glass, not only to reduce glare but to provide a continually changing pattern of reflections to the atrium walls; and to add to the appearance at night by means of 12 volt spots concealed in the sills of the bedroom windows, lighting upwards to the roof. The spots add a starlight appearance to the space at night.

The main dining room
By developing a lightwell in the older 1884 part of the building, this allowed a daylight rooflight to be introduced into the building at a position central to the main restaurant. The rooflight is a flamboyant design which fits well with the hotel's antecedents.

Whilst clearly the amount of daylight available is insufficient for everyday restaurant use, it does mean that during the day the room has an impression of being lit by natural light even on dull days, an important aspect particularly at breakfast, whilst on bright days the amount of natural light is significant.

The bedrooms
The number of bedrooms was increased from 140 to 270, making the whole project viable.

By stripping off the existing roof and mansard floor, it enabled this to be replaced by a new copper mansard, containing two to three floors. Each of the rooms were given a quality or character, particular to the hotel period, whilst in some cases balconies were provided.

Daylight was of the essence, to provide an atmosphere very different from the standard London hotel, where possible with views out towards London. It is hard to know whether the guests will be impressed by this, but it must have some impact on the question of energy control, a subject which may have more meaning in the future. It is important to know that daylight has informed the design.

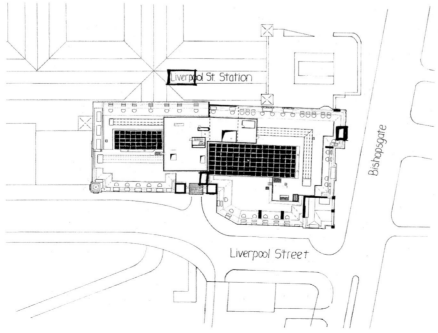

The Manser Practice

Site Plan

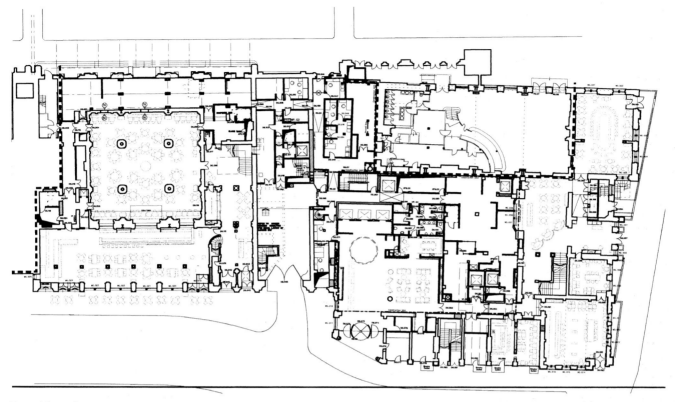

Ground floor plan

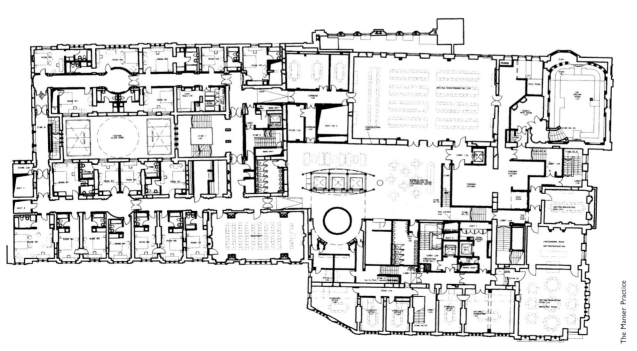

First floor plan

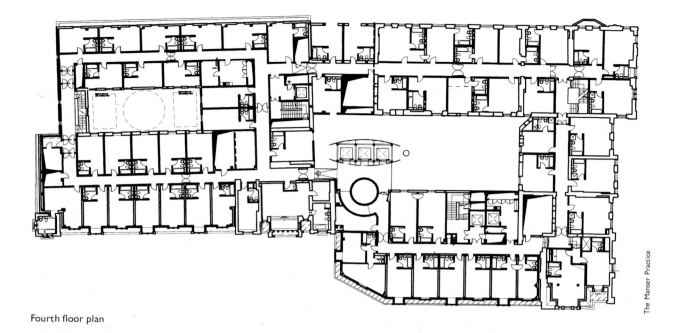

Fourth floor plan

The Manser Practice

Entrance lobby with circular light well

DP Archive

View down the circular lightwell

DP Archive

Atrium with view up to glazed ceiling/night

Roof detail

DP Archive

The main dining room

Peter Cook/View

View of the glass rooflight in the dining room

DP Archive

Roof and window detail

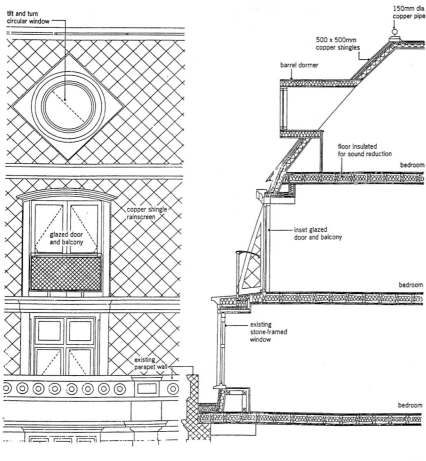

tilt and turn
circular window

150mm dia
copper pipe

500 x 500mm
copper shingles

barrel dormer

copper shingle
rainscreen

glazed door
and balcony

floor insulated
for sound reduction

bedroom

inset glazed
door and balcony

bedroom

existing
stone-framed
window

existing
parapet wall

bedroom

2 March 2000

Manser Practice

Typical bedroom

Peter Cook/View

De Syllas House

Architect and client	Justin De Syllas, Avanti Architects
Lighting design	Justin de Syllas

First House, Dartmouth Park Road in London, was built by the architect Justin De Syllas for his own use, and shows a careful use of daylighting in informing the space.

The house is placed across the front of the site, which measures 15 by 15 m and has been designed to provide a strong street presence, and to create a wide south facing façade to a garden at the rear.

The architect's stated ambition to provide a large open-plan living area, full of space and light, was the main motivation for the design for the house, leading to the first floor living room, with its open plan covering the entire area save the void for the double height to the dining room below.

The living area is associated with a wide terrace along the entire length of the building, connected to the living area by means of full height windows to the south with low level sills. To the north a large window located above the front door ensures that natural light enters the space from different directions, ensuring sunlight penetration at all times of the day.

The dining/kitchen is a double height space, with an open tread stair leading up to the first floor; it has a large bay window which connects to a dining patio. The combination of the bay window at low level and a large rooflight above gives the double height space its naturally lit quality at both levels.

The bedrooms, bathroom and study are located below the living room. These rooms are slightly raised over a basement, so that the main bedroom and study have french windows overlooking the garden; and the spare bedroom and bathroom have small windows overlooking the street, just above eye level to give privacy.

The house is provided with a number of energy saving measures not least of which are its daylighting credentials. The area of glazing to the south is considerable, providing solar heating in the winter, with limited window area to the north to conserve heat. At no time would artificial light be required during the day. The windows to the south are controlled by external awnings against solar gain and all may be opened to achieve summer ventilation.

Ground floor plan

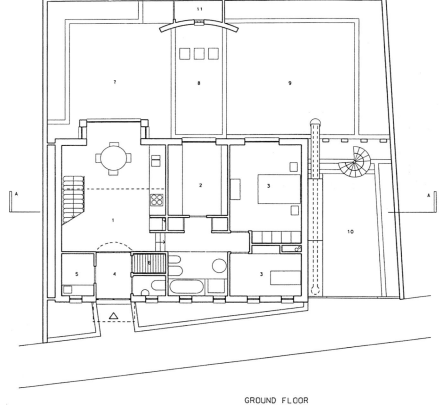

GROUND FLOOR

Justin De Syllas

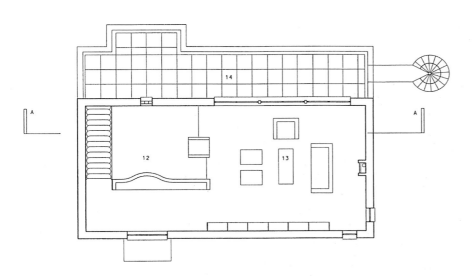

First floor plan

FIRST FLOOR

Justin De Syllas

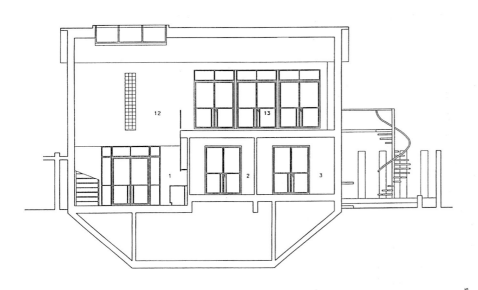

Long section

SECTION A–A

Justin De Syllas

Cross section

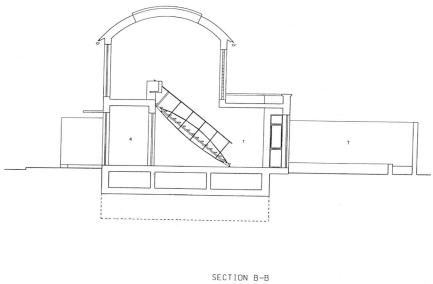

SECTION B-B

Justin De Syllas

Front elevation of the house

John E. Lindon

Interior of the living room to show the rooflight

John E. Lindon

Run of windows to the terrace from the living room

John E. Lindon

EDUCATION

Worlds End School, Enfield

Architect	Architects' Co-Partnership (ACP)
Engineer	TG Armstrong and Partners
Client	London Borough of Enfield

The secondary school at Enfield was a typical PFI project, built by contractors Laing Ltd with designs by architects ACP. The classroom designs had to meet the requirements of the London Borough of Enfield, where the illumination levels required were given as 300-500 lux, depending upon the activity within.

The enclosed plans indicate an E-shaped configuration of classrooms with daylight entering from windows either side, with a linear pitched rooflight down the centre to balance the daylight.

Each classroom had to be designed to a specific floor area requirement, which

resulted in a structural grid size of 7.5 m by 7.5 m being determined.

A further daylighting requirement suggested that the depth of all classrooms should not exceed 7 m. The room heights were standardized at 2.985 m, with a cill height of 0.95 m in order to ensure that the

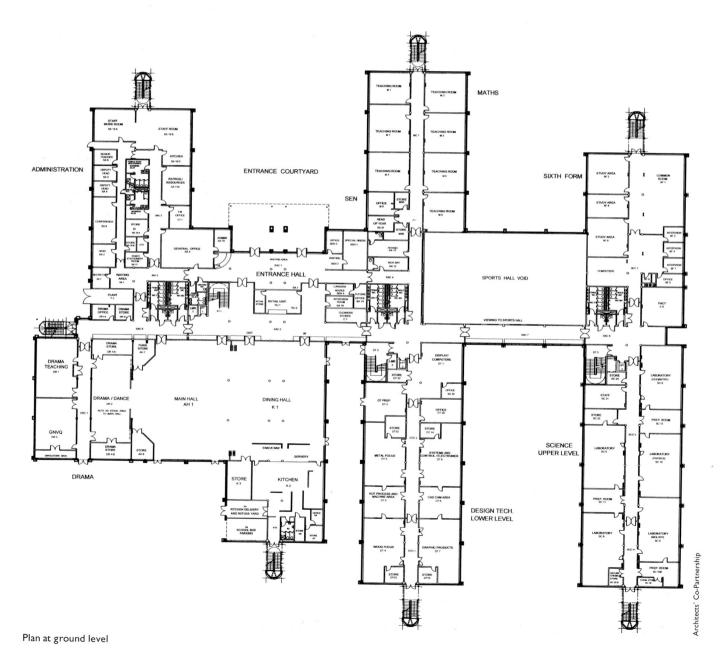

Plan at ground level

Architects' Co-Partnership

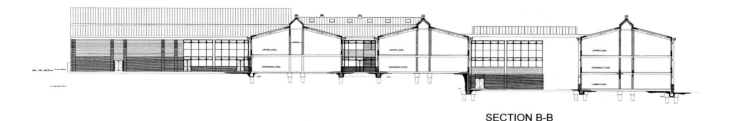

SECTION B-B

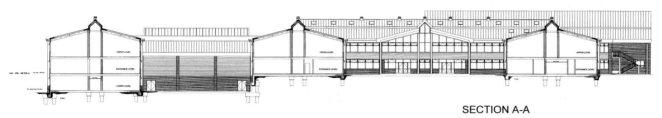

SECTION A-A

Section to show classroom wings and rooflight

Architects' Co-Partnership

amount of available daylight would reach the minimum standards set. This led to a window area of 65 per cent of the external wall.

Windows are double glazed, with the external pane comprising low emissivity 'grey' tinted glass, to reduce solar gain. Windows to the south, west and east have all been fitted with internal blinds between the double glazed panes, to provide individual control when required. Ventilation is achieved by top hung opening lights.

The engineers provided a daylight analysis for the sports hall, which indicated an average daylight factor of 3.8 per cent from a small area of overhead daylighting, which whilst lower than Ministry guidelines, was thought to provide 300 lux over the floor area for 75 per cent of daylight hours.

The control of the artificial lighting is by manual switching in the individual areas; since there is no BEMS there is no opportunity for daylight linking, and it is left very much up to

the person in charge of the classroom to make decisions as to whether the artificial lighting is required to supplement the daylighting at any particular time. Whilst savings in energy are in the hands of staff, the excellent daylighting allows savings in lighting energy to be made provided that there is determined management.

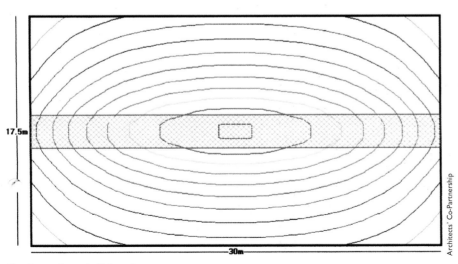

Architects' Co-Partnership

Illuminance from daylight only

External elevation, main entrance

Circulation, first floor

Architects' Co-Partnership

Sports hall

Architects' Co-Partnership

Orchard Learning and Resource Centre

Architect	Ahrends Burton and Koralek (ABK)
Engineer	Ove Arup and Partners
Client	Selly Oak Colleges, Cadbury Trust

The Orchard Learning and Resource Centre at Selly Oak contains a large library facility, with associated administrative offices and secure rooms for book storage, built in 1995 using a design and build contract, with contractor Tilbury Douglas.

The brief for the environmental design was written by Arups, who were responsible for the structural and environmental design, also thermal analysis, and after discussions with the architect, for the daylighting strategy and window design.

The strategy adopted resulted in a passive solar building with natural ventilation, with the elimination of an overall air-conditioning system, with the exception of certain critical areas. The daylighting strategy was designed to reduce the use of energy as far as possible.

The form of the building seen in the accompanying plans consists of three interlinked modules, with a linear skylight running the full length of the building, giving daylight through to the ground floor by what might be described as an atrium. The building is on an east/west axis. The critical south elevation is mastered by an existing row of deciduous trees, which provide desirable solar shading during the summer months, whilst allowing maximum sunlight through in the winter.

The library open plan areas are naturally ventilated and receive daylight both from the side windows and the central atrium. The projecting bays at first floor level provide very attractive study areas on the north side of the building. What is most important is that there is an overall environment of daylight during the day, giving the building its special quality.

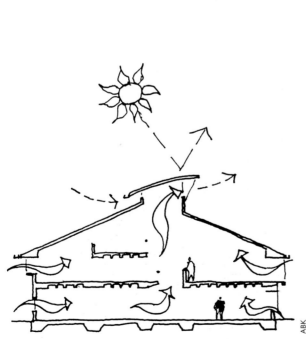

Sketch section to show ventilation system, with windows and skylight

Sketch section through the atrium

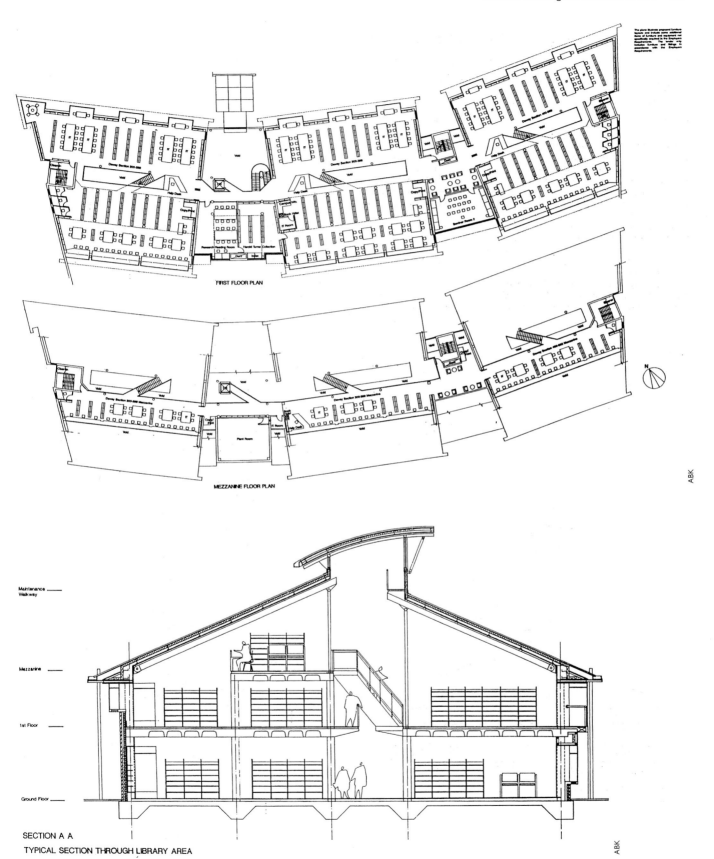

FIRST FLOOR PLAN

MEZZANINE FLOOR PLAN

ABK

Maintenance
Walkway

Mezzanine

1st Floor

Ground Floor

SECTION A A

TYPICAL SECTION THROUGH LIBRARY AREA

Plans at ground, first and mezzanine level

ABK

NORTH ELEVATION

North elevation

ABK

North elevation to show the projecting bays

DP Archive

Interior of the library area

Clerestorey glazing at high level with catwalk for maintenance

Students Union, University of Warwick

Architect	Casson Conder
Engineer	Buro Happold
Client	University of Warwick

The project arose from a decision made by the University that additional space was needed for the existing Students Union Building, due to the increasing number of students, and the need to provide many facilities which had not been available in the past.

The existing building had, in addition to a number of large spaces suitable for social activities, all the Students Union administrative offices. It was agreed to develop the larger spaces for students'

activities, but to remove all the administrative offices to the new building.

A number of retail services were to be provided to include a supermarket, post office, print shop and bar/restaurant.

After discussions with Buro Happold a decision was made that these latter facilities, where good daylighting was less essential should be placed at the ground level; whilst the offices and leisure rooms should be located on two upper levels where good daylighting

could be provided by both side windows and overhead roof lighting. This solution permitted an environmentally friendly building, where the energy used for artificial lighting during the day could be minimized.

The section and accompanying first floor plan shows the introduction of a central atrium running the length of the building, which provides maximum daylight through a sloping glass roof coupled with clerestorey lighting.

The daylight penetrates from the top down to the first floor level. Side daylighting enters from both the south and the north elevations, with additional *brise soleil* to the south to control sunlight, and light shelves at the first and second levels to light upwards to the ceilings.

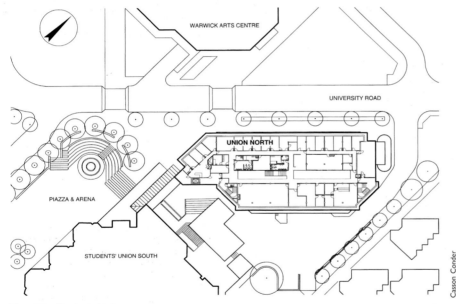

Plan of the Students Union

Casson Conder

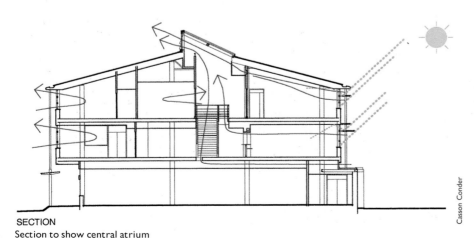

SECTION
Section to show central atrium

Casson Conder

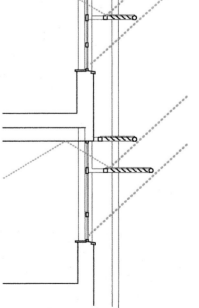

DETAIL SECTION
Section through window to show solar shielding

Casson Conder

Building exterior, daylight

Daylighting to the atrium from roof level

Interior of one of the upper floor leisure areas

Atrium from first floor level

The accommodation at first and second floor levels is lit from the South by windows and the central atrium, whilst the accommodaton to the north has an internal corridor with rooms doubled up, lit either from the north side or the central atrium.

The resulting solution ensures that the central area of the two upper floors are well daylit, and even catch some sunlight during certain hours of the day. The sun is not controlled by blinds and there is perhaps some danger of overheating from the overhead sun, though this would be rare in the UK.

Energy studies were carried out by Buro Happold, and a system of daylight linking by means of photocells, adopted to ensure that the level of artificial light is controlled during the day, and can be related to the level of the outside daylight. There is no Building Management System (BEMS) to provide a more direct control, but despite this, an economic energy solution has been provided.

City Learning Centre, Bristol

Architect	Alec French Partnership
Engineer	Wicheloe MacFarlane BDP
Client	Bristol City Council and Excellence in Cities

The City Learning Centre at Monks Parks in Bristol is one of a series of Centres designed by the architects, Alec French Partnership, as a part of the Government's Excellence in Cities initiative, designed to provide specialist cutting edge ICT facilities for Bristol City Council.

The buildings were commissioned in February 2001 and completed in December, being designed to provide high quality stimulating environments for both the studious and the disaffected.

The lighting strategy for the building was as follows:

- To provide comfortably lit learning environments suitable for the use of computers

- To maximize the use of natural light, whilst minimizing solar gain
- To engage the circulation and social spaces with the outside environment
- To allow the users to be aware of changes in the weather and seasons.

A glance at the plans and sections indicate how these objectives have been achieved. The organization of the building is immediately understandable on entry into the central area, with its open top lit staircase. The extensive use of 'Kalwall' translucent cladding for the first floor walls allows high levels of natural light, whilst avoiding glare to the VDUs (see also the Chelsea Club, pp. 148–151). At ground floor level more traditional windows allow views out from the café and circulation areas.

The environment created within the teaching spaces by the translucent glazing at first floor level provides a good level of daylight without glare, whilst a sequential change is made by the movement of the sun and the weather as it impinges on the exterior cladding. At night the walls appear translucent, giving a characteristic appearance when in use, which establishes the building in its setting.

The glazed angled projecting café provides daylight and views out linking the building clearly to its context, whilst solar gain is controlled by a series of horizontal oak louvres.

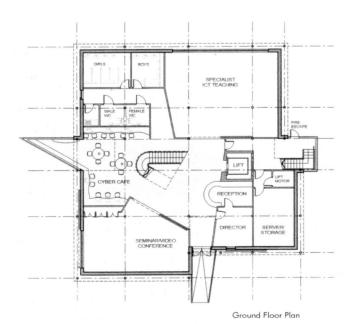

Ground floor plan

First floor plan

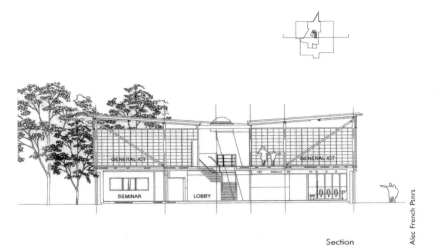

Section

Alec French Ptnrs

Section

Exterior

DP Archive

Typical teaching area showing the translucent wall

DP Archive

The view out from the projecting café

DP Archive

New Faculty of Education, UWE

Architect	Alec French Partnership
Engineer	Arup
Client	Bristol City Council

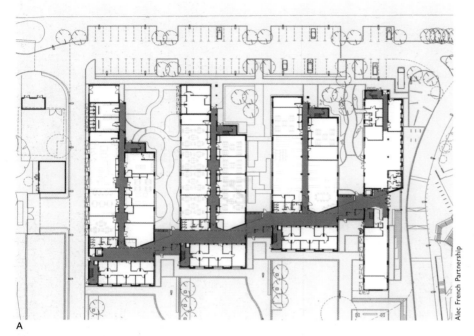

A

First Floor Plan

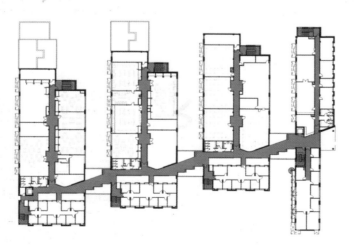

B

The plans showing the linkage of the street to the individual wings formed by the teaching areas.
A. Ground floor; B. First floor

The Faculty of Education was relocated to join the main UWE campus at Frenchay, outside Bristol, requiring the master planning and landscaping of an area to the south-west of the University campus. After discussion, it was agreed that the building should be modelled on a contemporary working environment, but at the same time the brief aspired to create a model teaching environment, incorporating all the facilities to be found in primary and secondary schools. There appeared to be no contradiction in these two scenarios.

The lighting strategy agreed was as follows:

- To provide appropriate levels of lighting for a range of teaching, administration and social spaces
- To make the most effective use of natural light to reduce running costs and CO_2 emissions, and to enjoy the varying qualities of the natural source
- To relate the building to its external environment and landscaping.

As can be gained from the diagrams, the large amount of space required by a University faculty is broken down into four wings connected by a double height social and communication space.

By breaking up the accommodation into a series of parallel wings the architect met the brief to provide naturally lit teaching spaces, whilst the interconnecting 'street' was unified by the overhead daylighting. The whole provides a very human environment.

The extensive use of controlled natural light in the teaching wings reduces the heat load and energy consumption of artificial lighting. Temperatures are allowed to fluctuate more widely in the street which acts as a passive solar modifier to the rest of the building.

The accompanying photographs show clearly the success of the double height street, together with the external spaces or courtyards between the wings as experienced from outside and within the building, meeting the brief for a unity between the internal/external environment and the landscaping.

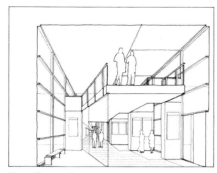

Street Perspective

Street Perspective

Two perspectives of the street

The street at ground level

The street at first floor level showing the rooflighting

The courtyard space between the wings

View of the courtyard from the interior

Polk County Science Centre

Architect	John McAslan and Partners
Lighting design	Arup
Client	Florida Southern University, Florida

The author visited Florida Southern University in 1952, shortly after the architect Frank Lloyd Wright had designed it; it had been an eye opener, for university buildings of the day, with Wright's fondness for natural light providing a user friendly campus, rich in exterior landscape. Now some 50 years later it has suffered from poor construction (Wright was not responsible for supervision of the work) and neglect and was desperately in need of rehabilitation. The work was carried out by John McAslan with Arup as engineers, Earl Walls as laboratory planners, and Lunz Prebor Fowler as executive architects.

In terms of daylighting there were three types of problem:

1. The central atrium which is naturally lit by east facing clerestorey glazing at high level
2. Laboratories which are naturally lit by east and west facing clerestory glazing at high level

3. Offices and seminar rooms naturally lit by full height glazing from a variety of orientations.

The daylighting problems were studied in model form.

Due to the orientation of the main run of buildings in a north–south direction, the early morning east sun and evening west sun entered the classrooms and laboratories directly, causing disruptive glare problems. Many of the windows had been covered with dark grey film to control the sun, and worse, were covered with forms of drape or blind cutting out the daylight.

The clerestorey glazing to the central atrium was inadequate to allow the natural light to filter down to the first level, rendering the building dim and inhospitable. In addition, the artificial lighting using tungsten sources was unable to compensate for the low levels of natural light. The window

glass was replaced with a light tinted product to minimize glare from the east and west sun, a colour balance being struck to ensure that this did not alter the exterior appearance of the building for historic purposes.

The original tungsten lighting which had been used throughout was replaced with modern energy efficient light sources, such as fluorescent. A combination of daylight, functional artificial lighting with some dramatic artificial sources was used. In this way improvements were made to the artificial lighting of the atrium, the laboratory and classrooms, together with the offices to ensure that all areas of the building were brought up to modern standards; however the needs of daylighting and its relationship with artificial sources was always a consideration, to retain as far as possible the original design intent of the world famous architect.

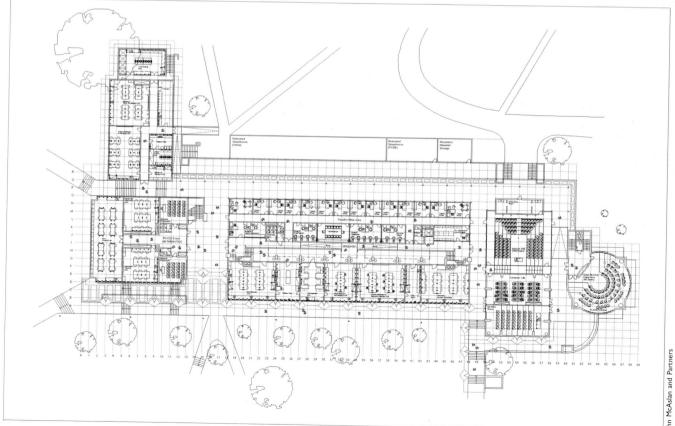

Ground plan

John McAslan and Partners

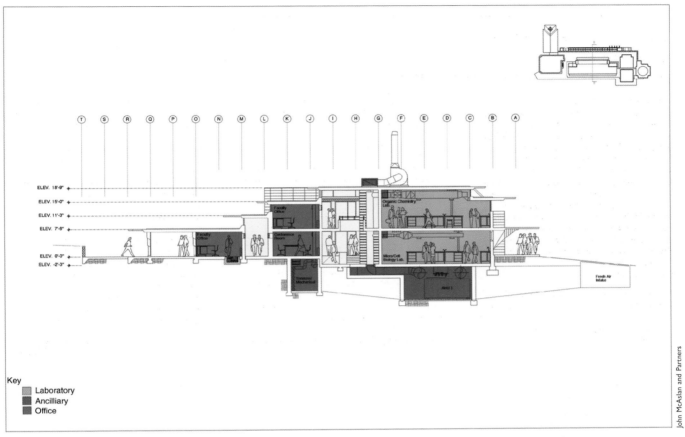

Key
- Laboratory
- Ancilliary
- Office

Section

John McAslan and Partners

Model of the section

John McAslan and Partners

The daylit atrium

The campus at night

Daylit corridor

Original solar shading by Frank Lloyd Wright

George Cott

Goldsmiths College

Architect	Allies and Morrison
Engineer	Max Fordham
Client	Goldsmiths College

The new Information Services Building at Goldsmiths College in New Cross, designed by the architects Allies and Morrison, provides a major extension to the college's paper-based library facilities, adding 2000 m² of flexible accommodation comprising information technology and language resource facilities.

The client's brief for the new building required its façade, which occupies a prominent position facing on to the A20 Lewisham Way, to present a new public front to the college and be a 'showpiece.' The architectural response was for the façade to be predominantly glazed thereby providing a highly visible view into the open plan of the building, which should be as impressive at night as during the day.

This approach required the designers to resolve the conflicting requirements of a highly glazed façade with the intensive useage of computer screens on the upper floors. This left them with three issues to address.

1. To overcome the practical problem of natural light entering the building and causing glare to the computer screens, control of 'sun glare' and reflections on to the VDUs.
2. To maximize the use of daylight, not only to allow views out of the building, but also to economize on the use of electrical energy for the artificial lighting.
3. To eliminate any heat gains from direct sunlight so that there should be no need for air-conditioning.

The solution adopted for the levels above ground floor on the north-east elevation consists of floor to ceiling clear glazing, with external vertical fins which not only control glare from the sun, but also allow generous external views. At night the impression of the building is of a luminous and transparent façade, thus fulfilling the client's brief.

Collaboration between the architects and consultants Max Fordham has produced an elegant and practical daylight solution to the problem posed by the universal adoption of computer screens (VDUs) when used adjacent to a completely glazed façade.

To control glare a series of external vertical fins or screens (*brise soleil*) have been fixed to the glazing. The exact nature of the fins resulted from model studies to determine the size and patterning of the holes required to give the required control, and the desired transparency. The metal fins have a 12 per cent free area, consisting of perforations on a grid of 10.9 by 15 mm. The finish of the fins

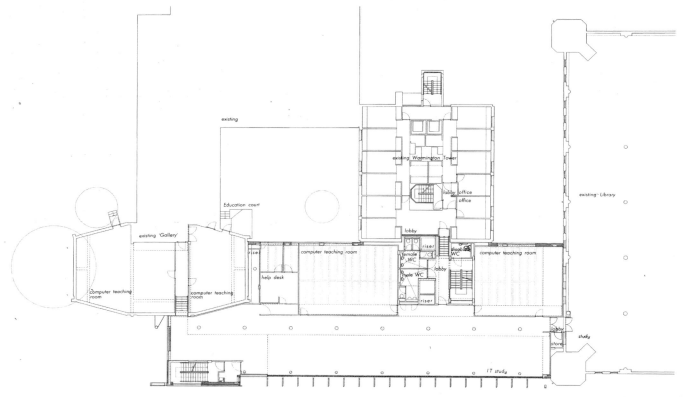

Plan at first floor level

Max Fordham

was carefully selected so that the colour intensity would not cause glare resulting from a marked contrast between the background natural light and the fin itself. Additionally the reflectivity of the finish should be relatively low to ensure that direct light was not reflected back into the building interior. This combination was found to solve the sun glare problem, whilst at the same time giving the appearance of transparency by allowing oblique views through.

Daylight levels are linked electronically with the artificial light by means of the BEMS which controls the supplementary artificial light when the daylight is insufficient. The method adopted is that the users switch the lights on when required, and the BEMS switches them off when daylight levels are suitable.

Artificial uplighting at the rear of the space consists of fluorescent lamps together with metal halides housed in a shelf beneath the ceiling; this light will be the first to come on followed by the central line of recessed downlighters, and finally the row of recessed lights closest to the window wall; in practice the latter are rarely needed.

The building requires no air-conditioning as it employs a system of displacement ventilation cooling. The supply air is introduced by a plenum method through circular steel registers set into the raised access floor. The combination of solutions to the lighting and ventilation satisfies the designer's desire for a holistic energy efficient solution.

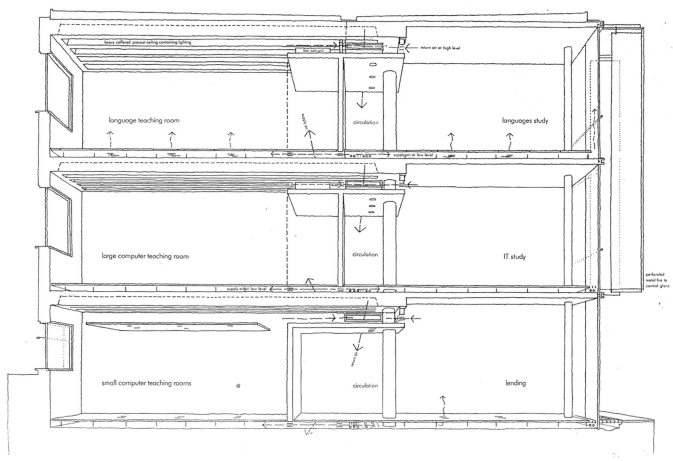

Section

Max Fordham

Exterior view during the day showing the fins

Interior view showing the layout and disposition of the computer screens

View out seen from the student's position

DP Archive

Detail of perforation to the fins

DP Archive

Michael Young Building, OU

Architect	Jestico+Whiles
Lighting consultant	Halcrow
Client	Open University

The Michael Young Building for the Open University Business School, was built at the Walton Hall Campus in Milton Keynes and completed in 2001. The building provides office and support accommodation for the staff originally occupying several temporary buildings on campus; in addition the building provides more meeting rooms with state of the art audio-visual facilities for the whole University.

The brief called for a low energy building designed to minimize maintenance and running costs. The BRE Method of Assessment (BREEAM) was used for environmental assessment during the design stage, and some modifications were made to achieve the highest levels, resulting in one of the highest scoring assessments made for any building.

The general strategy for the building can be seen from the plans, consisting of a simple H-Plan configuration of three storeys, consisting of a central core facilities block with four workspace wings radiating from it. The work spaces are designed to be as flexible as possible to facilitate a range of working configurations, such as cellular, group, or open plan.

The central core contains the vertical circulation, with an atrium giving access to the cafeteria. This central circulation area is designed to facilitate social interaction among staff and students .

The ventilation strategy for the building is closely related to the daylighting in that the method involved (Termodeck) demands that the window area does not not exceed 35 per cent glazing, resulting in lower Daylight Factors (DF) for the interiors. The workspace wings are orientated east/west to optimize solar gain, and to increase views out to the landscape, whilst limiting solar glare.

The general principle for the lighting is that the maximum use is made of available daylight with a system of daylight linking. When the artificial lighting is required (if there is an absence of natural light during the day) it will be automatically dimmed in response to an improvement in the local daylight level. Furthermore lights local to each work station can be turned on by clicking a special screen icon on their PC, with the light level being capable of being adjusted. Proximity switches automatically switch the artificial lights off after 15 minutes when no-one is there.

The final solution to the building, with its apparent success in terms of energy use, will be closely monitored for the first two years of occupation to ensure that the design intent is being delivered, with monthly energy reports being posted on the building's website.

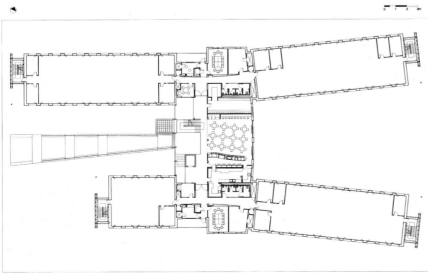

Open University Business School, Walton Drive, Milton Keynes   Ground Floor Plan   JESTICO + WHILES

Plan at ground level

Open University Business School, Walton Drive, Milton Keynes   First Floor Plan   JESTICO + WHILES

Plan at first floor level

Jestico+Whiles Architects

Jestico+Whiles Architects

The entrance atrium and reception

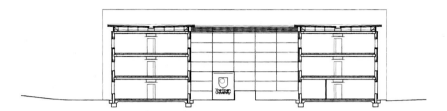

Section through Workspace (A)

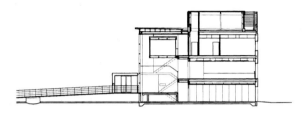

Section through Atrium (B)

Open University Business School, Milton Keynes   Sections

The central atrium

General view of the complex

The boardroom

Riverhead School, Sevenoaks

Architect	Architects Design Partnership
Lighting consultant	Slender Winter Partnership
Client	Kent County Council

The Riverhead School is a replacement for an old Victorian school supplemented by temporary classrooms. Built in 2001 by Architects Design Partnership, it was designed to be a 'green building' to fit into the landscape, and to be both educationally and environmentally responsive. The school is designed to house 270 pupils, and is not thought to require future expansion.

The complex is approached from the north side, which houses the entrance, and contains the service areas of the building, with space for the arrival and parking of cars.

The form of the building consists of an arch section facing south housing all the teaching areas. The roof fits into the landscape by being covered in vegetation. Originally designed to be covered in grass, a decision was made to use 'Sedum' to save weight and the associated structure cost.

The teaching classrooms open to the south on to landscaped areas, and are all daylit by means of the window walls, associated with circular rooflights to the rear of the spaces. The classrooms open out on to external teaching spaces, and these are divided up by removable canvas 'sails' which are stretched across between the classrooms; these provide both privacy and protection, advice being sought from an environmental audit by the Building Research Establishment at an early stage of the design.

Air freshness is a particular concern in classrooms, and when it is too cool or windy to open up the glazed double doors, vents are available above the doorheads, together with the openable rooflight to provide air movement. The curved section of the building assists in which the ceiling rises towards the rooflight, similar to the useful ventilation volume provided by the traditional high ceiling of the Victorian schoolroom.

The design meets the requirement to provide an environmentally responsive building, with an excellence of environment in which daylight plays an important part.

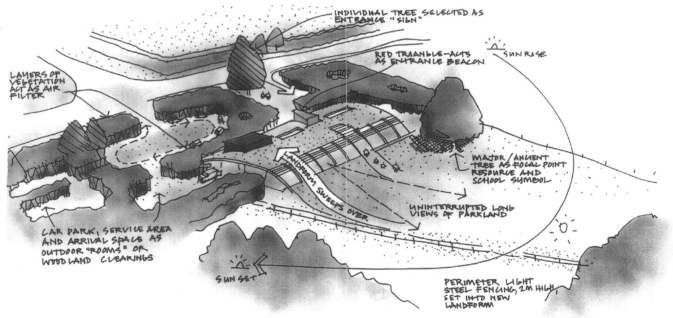

Architect's perspective to show the building concept

Architects Design Partnership

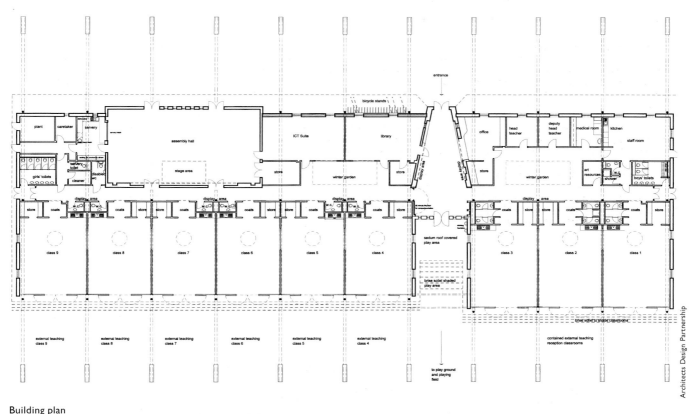

Building plan

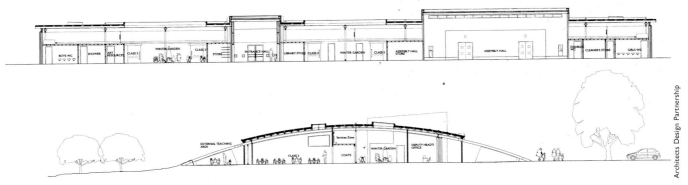

Building sections

Architects Design Partnership

View of the school from the south, classroom side

Ray Hardinge

View to the south from the interior of a classroom

Ray Hardinge

View of a classroom towards the rear, showing the effect of the daylighting and the circular rooflight.

Ray Hardinge

ECCLESIASTICAL

Central United Methodist Church, Milwaukee, Wisconsin

Architect	William Wenzler and Associates
Lighting consultant	William Lam and Associates
Client	Central United Methodist Church

The Methodist Church built in Milwaukee by architects William Wenzler Associates was completed in 1982. The church is partly submerged into a hillside, with the roof being formed by the hillside itself and covered in wild flowers. The climate in the area is cold and by forming the church, sheltered by earth on three sides, it is protected to minimize operating costs.

The nave is surrounded by ancillary spaces, but the architect resisted the temptation to incorporate perimeter skylights in his design, as this would have prejudiced the simplicity of the effect of the wild flowers on the hillside, so that another solution had to be found. This solution consists of a tall tower with sunlight entering from the south, with a blank wall to the north.

The tall tower which can be seen in the photograph is designed to collect both light and solar energy, but also registers the presence of the church in the neighbourhood; it bears a resemblance to Utzon's Bagsvaerd Church in Denmark, although for somewhat different reasons (*Lighting Modern Buildings*, Case Study 8, pp. 118/9).

The tower contains an electrically operated high-tech thermal shutter which can track the sun, offering an inexpensive opportunity for redirecting low angle winter sunlight towards the floor of the chancel, whilst at the same time directing some light to the roof of the nave, by means of a secondary system of mirrors below.

During the summer the shutter is in its closed position to reject high angle summer sunlight and heat.

In order to test the system, model studies were carried out to convince the architect that the idea was practical. This is an excellent use of model studies which can be carried out quite simply using actual sunlight conditions; they are both quicker and cheaper than to try to use the various methods of calculation or by means of computers. The model studies showed the architect the dramatic sunlight patterns that would be achieved. The photographs of the actual interiors shown here followed the model studies closely.

Whilst no daylight is received directly to the nave, by the traditional means of aisle and clerestorey lighting, the solution adopted for controlling the daylight and sunlight from the tower, provides the theatrical impression required.

Plan

William Wenzler Associates

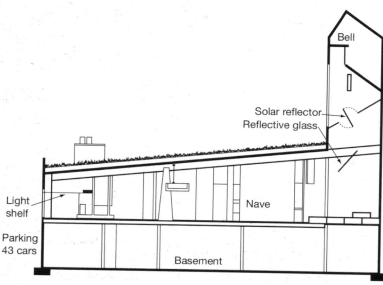

Section built into hillside

William Wenzler Associates

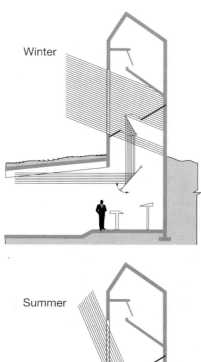

Winter

Summer

Section through tower. Winter/Summer

William Wenzler Associates

The tower.

William Lam

Interior of the chancel

William Lam

Interior of the nave

William Lam

Rothko Chapel, Houston

Architect	Philip Johnson, followed by Barnstone and Aubry
	Restoration by Jim McReynolds Architects
Lighting consultant	Arup Lighting
Client	Menil Foundation

The Rothko Chapel was built on a plot adjacent to the Menil Collection in Houston, Texas, to house a collection of paintings by Mark Rothko, and opened in 1971. By the 1990s the chapel was in a bad state of repair. The paintings themselves had deteriorated, and a decision was made to take the opportunity, whilst repairs were made to the structure, to employ consultants to introduce a new scheme for both daylighting and artificial lighting to ensure the long term future of the paintings.

The brief to the consultants, Arup Lighting, was to propose alterations both to lengthen the life of the paintings, and to improve the quality of space for the visitors.

This Case Study is concerned with the natural lighting, with the following brief:

1. To study the existing conditions regarding the amount of daylight and sunlight to which the paintings are exposed.

2. To consider whether this exposure is excessive, in terms of the conservation of the work.

3. To study the visual perception by the visitors, to assess whether the distribution of both daylight and sunlight is impairing the view of the works of art.

The results of this enquiry would pinpoint any shortfalls in the existing daylighting design, and led to suggestions as to how they might be overcome. An extensive survey with both computer and physical models was conducted, and the results showed that the levels of sunlight penetration had been the cause of deterioration in the paintings, and that the daylight distribution caused unsatisfactory viewing conditions for the visitors. New proposals were essential.

By a process of elimination a decision was made that the sunlight entering the space from the existing rooflight should be diffuse and scattered, rather than blocked, and that

this could be achieved by diffuse laminated glass with a milky white opal PVB interlayer. The incoming sunlight would no longer have directionality, but an internal fixed shading element would still be required to reduce the quantity of natural light and to avoid the bright skylight becoming a distraction to the visitors, whilst at the same time assisting in directing the light to improve the uniformity to the light received by the paintings.

After a number of options were investigated, this was achieved by a dropped baffle, small enough to allow the full height of the paintings to receive direct daylight, with the addition of a central 'oculus' to provide some daylight to the centre of the space.

The final result can be seen in the accompanying photographs, and this has proved to be well received by the public, whilst obviating future deterioration in the paintings.

The exterior of the chapel after restoration in 2000

View of the new rooflight, 2000

Jeff Shaw, Arup Lighting

View of the dropped baffle as installed in 2000

Hickey-Robertson

Interior of the space after the restoration and the new daylighting scheme had been installed

LEISURE

Chipping Norton Leisure Centre

Architect   Fielden Clegg Bradley
Lighting consultant   Brian Ford Associates
Client   West Oxfordshire District Council

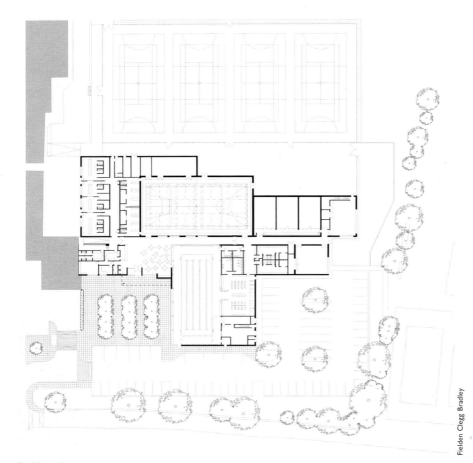

Building plan

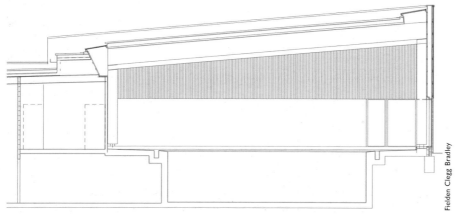

Section through swimming pool

The Chipping Norton Leisure Centre is a dual use facility completed in 2002. It contains a 25 m × 4 lane swimming pool, a four-court sports hall, fitness suite, dance studio and three squash courts.

Computer and physical modelling of the proposed daylight solutions was explored, the final solution allowing the sports hall and swimming pool to operate in daylight hours without the need for artificial lighting.

An analysis of the daylight conditions in the sports hall and swimming pool were undertaken to determine both the quantity, distribution and quality of the daylight within these spaces for various rooflight and diffuser options. Annual energy use, energy costs and CO_2 emissions, related to the artificial lighting requirements, were also estimated for the different rooflight design options.

Since both computer and physical models were used for this work it is of interest to note that significant differences were found. Generally higher Daylight Factors (DF) were predicted using the physical models than those obtained from the computer, but the pattern of light distribution was found to be similar, and the visual effect of the various options could be assessed by the architects more readily with the physical models.

There were various reasons for the differences, perhaps the most significant being the imperfections at junctions in the model.

The resulting solutions may be seen in the photographs.

In the swimming pool the large windows down the west side of the pool make the most significant contribution, supplemented by the rooflights running the length of the pool on either side. The daylight design obviates the danger of reflections off the water from obscuring the view of swimmers in difficulties.

In the sports hall an entirely different approach is adopted by means of runs of overhead rooflights, controlled by fabric diffusers, which solve the problem of solar glare.

The success of the daylighting of the Chipping Norton Leisure Centre has resulted from the application of careful daylight studies, and the willingness to take the necessary time to apply the results of energy studies, thus ensuring a sustainable solution.

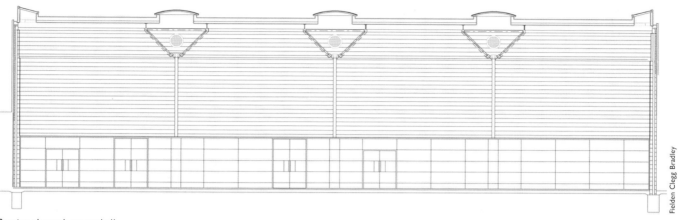

Fielden Clegg Bradley

Section through sports hall

Andrew Southall

Sports hall

Andrew Southall

Sports hall detail of fabric diffuser   Swimming pool

Andrew Southall

Chelsea Club and Chelsea World of Sport

Architect   Fletcher Priest

Services engineers   TME Engineers

Client   Chelsea Village

The Chelsea Club provides private sports facilities for its members, including a 25 m level deck swimming pool, 200 m running track at high level around the perimeter, sports injury clinic, cardiovascular and aerobic studios, jacuzzi, steam room and sauna; this is associated with the Chelsea football ground at Stamford Bridge. The top floor of the building houses the Chelsea World of Sport, an interactive exhibition explaining the relationship between physiological performance and sporting achievement. This is linked by a bridge to the adjacent stadium.

The use and mass of the building are clearly articulated. The main spaces are accommodated with two 3-storey blocks either side of a glazed link which brings daylight into the heart of the building and contains the central stair and glazed lift. High level *brise soleil* protect the south elevation from the sun. Escape stairs, lifts and main plant are concealed in louvred enclosures at either end of the building.

The lighting brief was unusual in that due to the need for privacy, views 'out from' and 'into' the facility were to be excluded, but the impression of a daylit space was desired.

The exterior impression of the building is of white wall cladding, whilst the interior reminds one of the effect of Japanese shoji screens, as a simple backroom to the working areas.

The appearance is gained from the use of vandal-resistant, light-diffusing fibreglass panels. This material, called 'Kalwall', which spans from floor to ceiling around the perimeter of the space allows daylight through to all the major spaces of the interior during the day, whilst at night it allows the artificial light from the interior, to spill out a glow to the exterior façade, obviating the need for any exterior floodlighting to register the form of the building.

The artificial lighting had to provide glarefree light to the interior, so as not to be disturbing to the members, some of whom may be carrying out exercises lying on their backs looking upwards to the ceiling. The solution adopted is to stretch membrane ceilings between the beams, which are back lit by concealed fluorescent lamps.

This solution, which is a method of daylight linking, is very successful providing a light level which can be varied from low for exercises such as yoga, to high levels where this is required. The combination of daylight received through the 'Kalwall' panels and variable artificial light from the stretched membrane panels provides a calm soft light with no hard shadows, ideal for the sporting activities below.

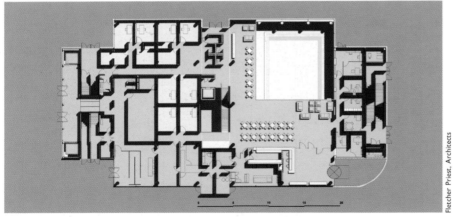

Plan

Fletcher Priest, Architects

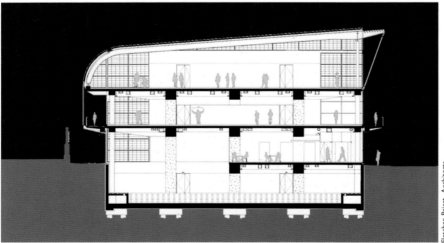

Section

Fletcher Priest, Architects

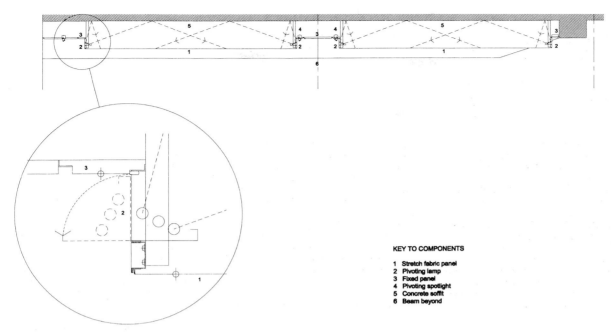

KEY TO COMPONENTS

1 Stretch fabric panel
2 Pivoting lamp
3 Fixed panel
4 Pivoting spotlight
5 Concrete soffit
6 Beam beyond

Detail of sketched membrane ceiling and lighting

Daylit exterior

Fletcher Priest, Architects

Chris Gascoigne/View

Exterior at night

Chris Gascoigne/View

Interior of a working space

Serpentine Gallery Pavilion

Architect	Toyo Ito
Engineers and lighting designers	Arup
Client	Serpentine Gallery

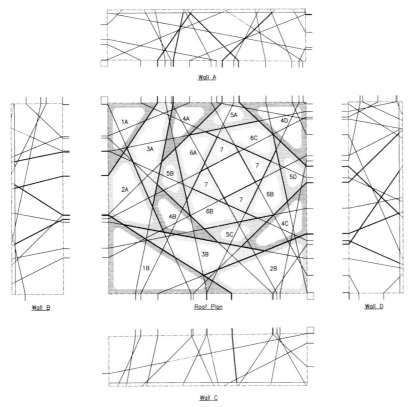

The wall and roof plans

The Pavilion in Kensington Gardens designed by Toyo Ito, can hardly be described as an exercise in daylighting design; however it has been included in the Case Studies, as daylight has clearly informed the architect's entire design. Perhaps the building is best described as an 'abstract work of art.'

The building is the third in a series of galleries commissioned to provide a unique showcase for contemporary architectural practice, following works by Zaha Hadid, and Daniel Libeskind, to design a pavilion for the gallery's lawn.

The purpose of the building was basically a restaurant during the day, and it is most successful in this, with views out on to Kensington Gardens, in which there is no need for artificial lighting.

In the evening the building is described by the sponsors as playing host to a special programme of summer events, architectural talks, film screenings and the BBC poetry proms, all requiring little or no artificial lighting. It can therefore be said that this project is entirely naturally lit. It is equally important to recognize that it is an ephemeral building, a 'statement' intended to be replaced the following year; it therefore required none of the limitations of having to withstand the test over time.

Since it would be difficult, if not impossible, to describe the pavilion adequately in words, it is best described in a series of photographs, which indicate the quality of the space, and the way in which it interacts on its surroundings in the park.

Exterior with entrance steps

Roof detail from inside

Exterior with entrance ramp

Detail of the exterior walling

Interior of the restaurant

American Community School, Sports Centre

Architect and lighting design   Studio E Architects

Client   American Community School, Cobham

The sports complex at the American School in Cobham is designed around two key areas : a 25 m pool and a sports hall to contain an international size basketball court. In addition a dance studio, fitness suite, café, and administration areas are provided at ground level, with changing rooms, and plant sunk at a lower level.

The pool hall has a north-westerly orientation, and this is exploited to allow for full height glazing on three sides, which provides both excellent daylighting and dramatic views of the surrounding woodland.

The orientation avoids low-level sun reflecting off the water resulting in a glare source to spectators and lifeguards. The daylighting consists of linear rooflights alternating with trapezoidal rooflights which permit sunlight directly into the pool. All glazing to the pool is low emissivity clear glass, to maximize daylight levels.

Whilst high levels of direct daylight are ideal for the pool, the sports hall requires a different approach, more controlled natural light suitable for ball games, and where views out are not justified. The roof form is similar to the pool hall, but the specification for the glazing is changed. The double glazed units use a grey solar glass for the outside panes to moderate the incoming light, and an opalescent glass on the inside for diffusion, even when the sun is shining directly on to it.

In addition clerestory windows and strip windows inset into the façade contribute to an evenly lit space. Low level sun is controlled by means of louvres to the perimeters of the pool and sports hall roofs.

The primary entrance level is open and transparent, with all spaces benefitting from natural light, making the addition of artificial light during the day unnecessary; whilst double-volume circulation spaces open up the changing-room level to allow natural light into the deepest areas of the building.

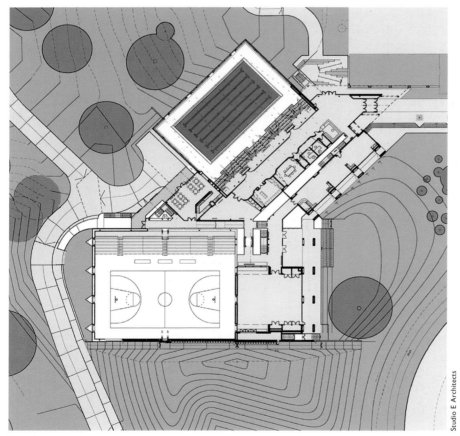

Studio E Architects

Site plan

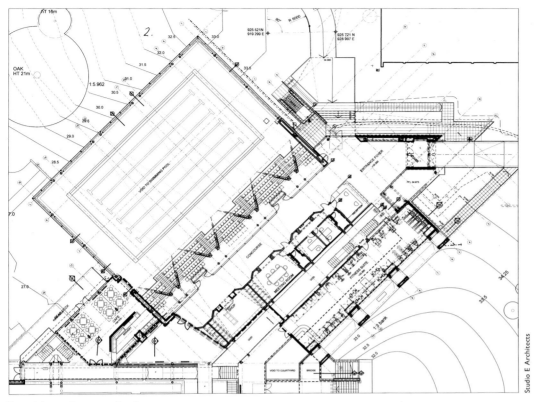

Plan of the pool entrance level

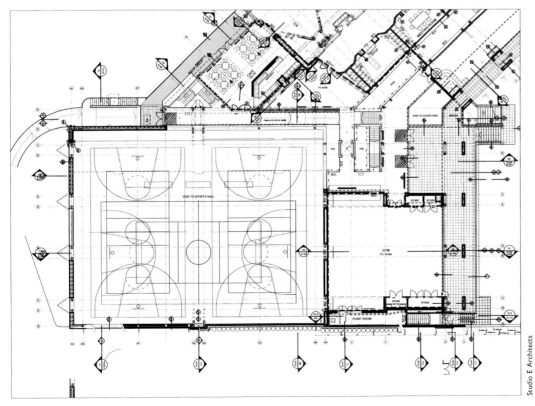

Plan of sports hall entrance level

General view of the pool

Andrzej Kuszell

View of roof at seating level

Andrzej Kuszell

View from side wall glazing to the pool

Sports hall general area

DISPLAY

Rooms at Royal Academy, Burlington House

Architect	R. Smitt, Surveyor to the Royal Academy of Arts
Lighting designer	DPA Lighting Consultants
Client	Royal Academy of Arts

In order to ensure that the Royal Academy keeps pace with the daylighting requirements of fine art galleries, the lecture room, together with a number of related spaces, were studied in terms of their daylighting control, on the assumption their existing glazed roof forms might be retained, but modified as needed.

The general brief for the daylighting was to provide a flexible and easily controlled system suitable for all of the top lit galleries, irrespective of their orientation which allows for the average daylight level to vary from nil to 500 lux or more. One of the important factors is the need to cater for 'indemnified exhibitions' or 'loan collections' where specific daylight levels are specified, from nil daylight to 300 lux, and where the gallery has a responsibility for its provision. This is different to the 'Summer collection', there for only a short period, and where it is not too important if the general level of daylight specified varies upwards on occasions.

After model studies were made the lighting consultants suggested a four-part solution, which was applied to the large lecture room, but formed the basis for a unified system which might be applied to a series of related areas.

The system is shown in the diagram below and consists of four layers:

1. The outer layer is a black tarpaulin supported on stainless steel suspension wires. This is installed manually on those occasions when a complete blackout is desired. The system is not used on a day to day basis.
2. External motorized louvre blinds. Placed above the glazing to the roof, these are open to the atmosphere, and needed to be made to a high specification to withstand rain, snow and high winds. The blinds are linked to an automatic control system which is 'daylight linked' to react to the external level of light, allowing predetermined maximum daylight levels to be set, for the display areas below.

When the room is closed to the public the blinds can be closed to reduce the daylight level, in order to minimize degradation of the exhibits.
3. The internal face of the glass to the rooflight is protected by a diffuse privacy film. The film is designed to match that used in the other galleries. The film provides both safety and anti UV control as well as diffusing direct sunlight.
4. The lowest level of control is formed by motorized and tensioned blinds formed of white close-weave fabric, each half of the sloping roof being separately controlled. The blinds can be seen by the public, and can either allow maximum daylight through, when open, or reduce the amount by adding a further degree of diffusion of the light to the space below.

The design intent has been met within a realistic budget, to provide the flexibility necessary to satisfy the needs of daylighting in different types of exhibition, whilst allowing a quick turnround time between one to another, by means of the simplicity of control.

1. *External Tarpaulin*
2. *External Motorized blinds*
3. *Diffuse privacy film in rooflight*
4. *Internal motorized, tensioned blinds*

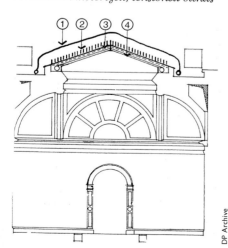

Interior during the day, using controlled daylight for an exhibition

View up to rooflight

Picture of the model used to establish the daylight factors

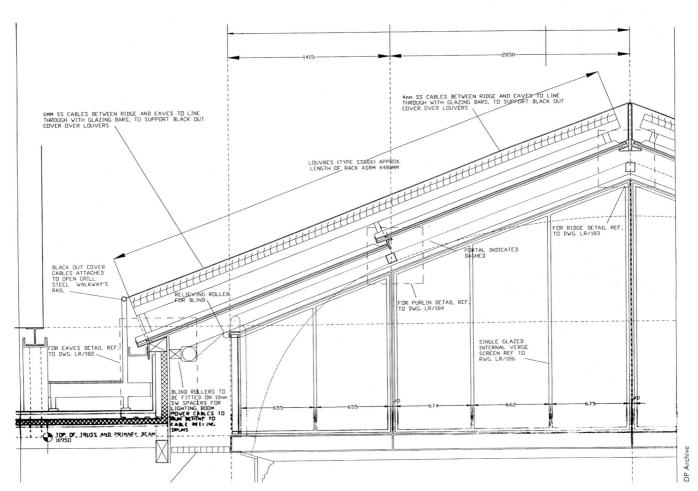

6MM SS CABLES BETWEEN RIDGE AND EAVES TO LINE THROUGH WITH GLAZING BARS, TO SUPPORT BLACK OUT COVER OVER LOUVERS

4mm SS CABLES BETWEEN RIDGE AND EAVES TO LINE THROUGH WITH GLAZING BARS, TO SUPPORT BLACK OUT COVER OVER LOUVERS

LOUVRES (TYPE SS80X) APPROX. LENGTH OF RACK ASRM 4480MM

FOR RIDGE DETAIL REF. TO DWG. LR/183

PORTAL INDICATED DASHED

BLACK OUT COVER CABLES ATTACHED TO OPEN GRILL STEEL WALKWAY'S RAIL

RELIEVING ROLLER FOR BLIND

FOR PURLIN DETAIL REF. TO DWG. LR/184

SINGLE GLAZED INTERNAL VERGE SCREEN REF TO RWG. LR/186

FOR EAVES DETAIL REF. TO DWG. LR/182

BLIND ROLLERS TO BE FITTED ON 10mm SW SPACERS FOR LIGHTING BOOM POWER CABLES TO RUN BEHIND TO CABLE REELING DRUMS

TOP OF TRUSS AND PRIMARY BEAM 10950

1415   2050

655   655   674   662   675

Drawing of the section through the rooflight to show the details of the different elements

Sainsbury, Greenwich

Architect   Chetwood Associates

Lighting Consultants   Pinniger and Partners

Client   Sainsbury's Supermarkets

The brief to the lighting consultants, working in close liaison with the m&e consultants, Faber Maunsell, was to develop 'an environmentally responsible lighting scheme,' in which the natural and artificial lighting would be closely integrated.

The building was designed by the architects, Chetwood Associates as the lowest energy supermarket, 50 per cent lower than conventional stores. The daylighting was achieved by an innovative roof design, incorporating eight high-angled north-facing rooflights, arranged in a sawtooth pattern occupying 20 per cent of the roof area. The daylighting design results in a high daylight factor (DF) of between 5 and 9 per cent.

Each window is equipped with motorized aluminium louvres, operated by photo-sensor control, specified by Faber Maunsell. These measure the available daylight and floor illuminance levels, opening and closing as required. At dusk they close completely, preventing upward spill light which would otherwise result in 'light pollution'.

The final result is an excellent combination of natural with artificial light, the natural light providing the general impression of the store being daylit; with the artificial light concentrated on providing the individual light to the goods, as specified by Sainsbury to be 1000 lux on the vertical services of the gondolas.

The vertical light is provided by luminaires mounted on specially designed brackets from the gondolas.

The store was completed in October 1999, described as the 'Millenium Superstore' it is a great credit to the client in initiating the concept of a 'daylit store,' associated with a low energy artificial lighting solution. The energy used for the artificial lighting has been stated as 25 watts/m^2, in a situation where the intangible value of the daylit interior of the store makes it a unique solution.

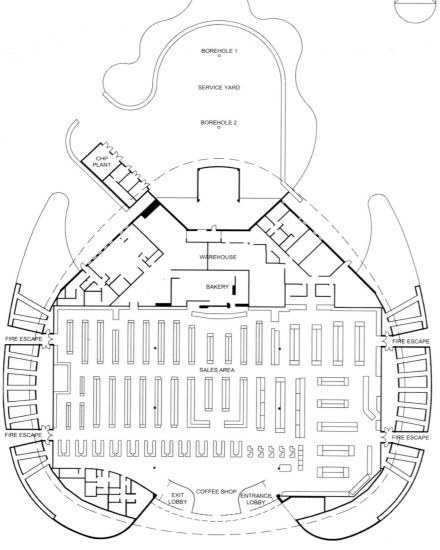

SAINSBURY'S AT GREENWICH PENINSULA   BUILDING PLAN

Chetwood Associates Architects

Plan of the store

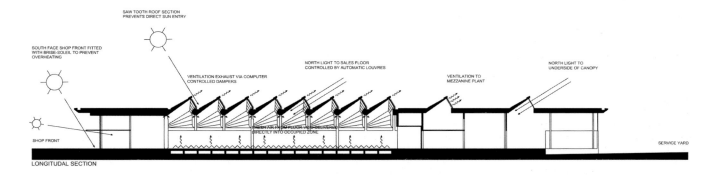

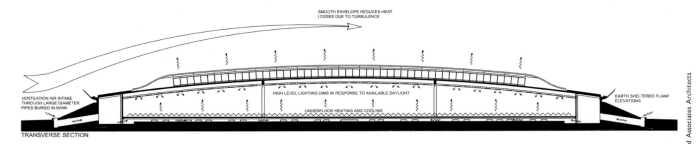

SAINSBURY'S AT GREENWICH PENINSULA   BUILDING SECTIONS

Cross and long sections

Chetwood Associates Architects

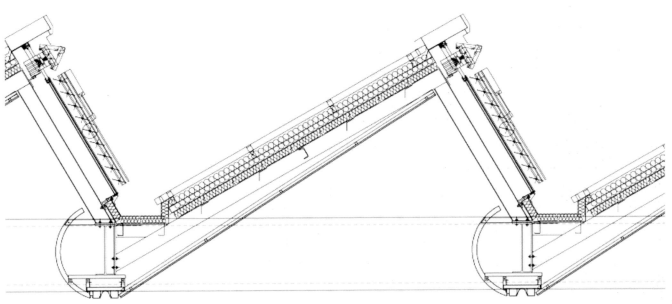

SAINSBURY'S AT GREENWICH PENINSULA   NORTHLIGHT DETAIL

Detail through the roof, to show the contours of the northlights

Chetwood Associates Architects

The roof from above

Cloud Nine Photography

Pinniger and Partners

Exterior of the frontage

General view of roof lighting and gondola fittings

Pinniger and Partners

Detail of roof lighting

Pinniger and Partners

Pinniger and Partners

General view of the checkout area

Museum of Country Life, Ireland

Architects	Office of Public Works, Dublin
Engineer	Sutton Vane Associates, Lighting Design
Client	Scroope Design, Dublin

Exterior of the building

View of the interior to show the window space contrasted with the low level display area

The Museum of Country Life at Turlough Park, Castlebar, in County Mayo is set in the landscaped grounds of a large country house in the West of Ireland, and as can be seen in the photograph below, it has large windows along the side elevations, in addition to the large end glazing.

The brief to the lighting designers was to utilize daylight, not so much to conserve energy, although it would have some effect on this, but to capitalize on the beautiful views out to the landscape through the windows.

The museum is designed to stress the importance of country life, so it is the setting for the way of life that created the artefacts to be shown in the museum. There was a desire to allow as much daylight in to the building consistent with the needs of conservation, so that the natural variation of daylight could be enjoyed, as it changes throughout the day and the seasons.

The building has large windows to the south-east and west, allowing both high levels of daylight, and direct sun penetration.

The problem presented to the lighting designer was therefore to provide an impression of natural light throughout the circulation areas of the building, whilst controlling the levels of light within the displays.

Several solutions were adopted: window film was applied to virtually every window to reduce the light levels overall, without destroying the view and where views were not important baffles were designed to direct light away from the artefacts, to the ceiling.

To solve the problem of sun penetration on the south and east elevations two-metre high screens parallel to the windows were placed in front of the display areas, giving the opportunity to the exhibition designer to create a low light level exhibition area within the limitation of 50 lux.

The layout of the building shows how the screens were placed, and this can be read in conjunction with the section to illustrate the the differentiation between the area lit by the windows for circulation, and the display area beyond with its low light level to ensure the conservation of the artefacts.

An exhibition of 'The Blacksmith'

Sutton Vane Associates

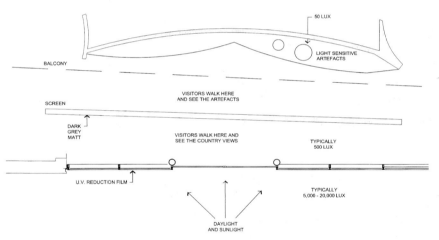

Plan of screening

Sutton Vane Associates

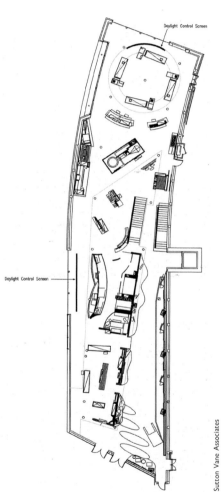

Typical plan of the 4-storey building

Sutton Vane Associates

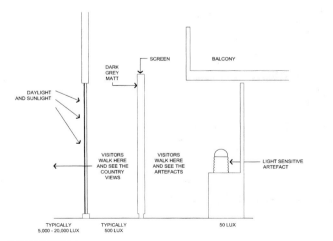

Section through the screening

Sutton Vane Associates

The Charioteer Statue, Archaeological Museum of Delphi

Architect	AN Tombazis and Associates
Lighting designers	London Metropolitan University (Prof. Mike Wilson and Andre Viljoen, with Bartenbach Lichtabor)
Client	Museum at Delphi

Many of the projects in this 'Display' section of Case Studies, are concerned with the display of a multitude of different objects; from food in a supermarket to the natural world; whereas in the case of the fifth century bronze Charioteer Statue at the Delphi Museum, the object of the exercise is to focus on to a single most important Greek statue.

The statue, which dates from 478 B.C. is of the Attic period, and is clearly the work of a major artist. The work has been housed in its own room in the museum, and the purpose of the daylighting design was to ensure that it should be seen as far as possible in the ever changing light of day, as the original artist would have seen it while carving the stone.

The original 'statue room' was lit on both side by clerestories, one of which was obstructed by an adjacent cliff face, limiting the daylight. The room was painted a light green which had the effect of reducing the impact of the natural verdigris on the bronze.

The impact of this was that the back of the statue was poorly lit, and that the strong vertical folds were poorly revealed.

Seventeen different roof configurations were investigated and tested under an artificial sky in order to find the optimum solution, whilst complementary heliodon studies indicated the need for shading devices to eliminate unwanted solar gains.

The initial concept for the room consisted of a circular rooflight located directly above the statue, but it was felt that this solution would not reveal the strong vertical character of the statue and the folds of the bronze (the David Statue in the Belle Arte Museum in Florence is lit in this manner. *Lighting Historic Buildings*, Architectural Press, p. 8.)

A number of the selected roof configurations were tested in a 1:18 scale model (the scale determined by available Charioteer souvenirs!) to determine the most appropriate means of daylight entry. The

chosen roof configuration incorporates a pyramidal roof structure with light shafts at 60 degrees, broad openings at roof level, and a 2 m by 2 m solid wedge directly above the statue itself. The daylight is diffused at roof level by transparent 'Okalux' which both diffuses the natural light and provides good insulation. Fans are mounted in the light shafts to extract unwanted solar gains.

A further development, which has proved very successful is the introduction of vertical screens in front of windows on three sides of the room. These screens which conceal the main window light, allow some indirect daylight to add variety to the faces of the interior walls, and provide a subdued framing to the statue on entering.

During the day the room is well daylit without any artificial light, with added artificial light at dusk. The aim is always to provide as natural appearance as possible.

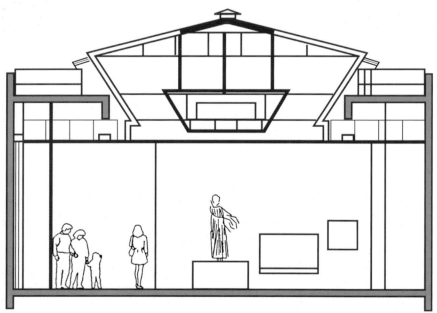

Cross section showing the chosen roof design

London Metropolitan University

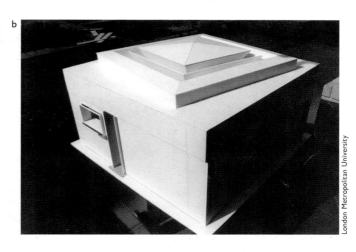

Photographs of the selected model a and b

Photographs of model c and d

The Charioteer as displayed in the Museum

General view of the room

Details of folds emphasized by the daylighting

Hong Kong Museum of Coastal Defence

Exhibition designer	ASL Dangerfield
Lighting designer	DPA Lighting Consultants
Client	Hong Kong Museum of History

Lei Yue Mun Museum
Hong Kong

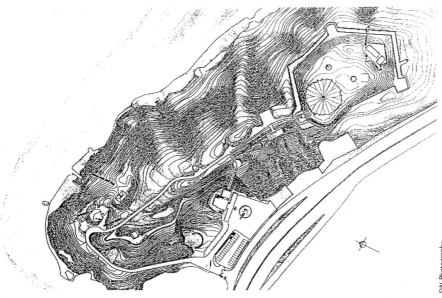

Location plan

The Redoubt at the Lei Yue Mun Museum in Hong Kong has a central courtyard, surrounded by a series of casemates (vaulted chambers) constructed in the ramparts of this former British fort. The courtyard and higher level are covered by a translucent roof membrane supported on four steel masts.

The brief to the lighting consultants required them to investigate the following aspects of the exhibition designer's responsibilities:

1. The way in which artificial lighting could enhance and dramatize a display in the courtyard in spite of the very high level of daylight.
2. The degree to which the daylight could penetrate the interiors of the casemates through the relatively narrow entrances from the courtyard, crucial knowledge when designing the display of fragile and fugitive artefacts.
3. The way in which the design of the exhibition fabric and lighting could help to overcome the problem of a visitor's adaptation to the different light levels on entering the casemates.
4. The design of the lighting within the casemates.

The enclosed character and artificial lighting of the exhibition proposed for the courtyard – a replication of a Chinese fort of the Qing dynasty – would have ensured a visually

SW Photography

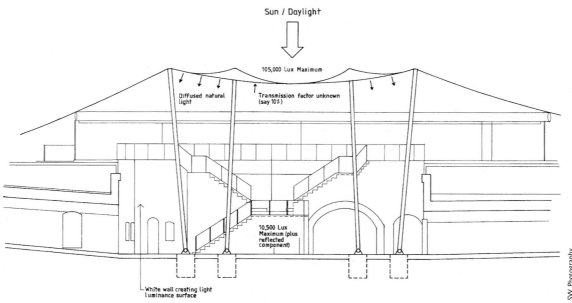

Section through the courtyard to show the location of the tentlike roof structure

SW Photography

exciting experience in spite of the abundance of daylight. In the event this proposal was abandoned in favour of a flexible assembly of large exhibits, and interactive video monitors.

To establish how much daylight would enter the casemates in terms of the percentage of natural light present in the courtyard, studies were carried out under the artificial sky at the Bartlett School of Architecture. This simulated the effect of the diffusing roof membrane.

Two studies were undertaken. The first was for a casemate with no obstruction to the daylight entering through the door opening. In spite of the introduction of a small obstruction within the casemate, the study demonstrated that natural light passing through a membrane with a 10 per cent transmission factor would produce a daylight factor (DF) of 1 per cent on the floor at the far end of the casemate, resulting in light levels far in excess of the 50 lux allowed. In a second study, an obstruction placed 1 metre inside the entrance resulted in substantially reduced daylight levels within the interior. Such obstructions, designed in various ways, allow for a variety of presentations of non-fugitive artefacts and graphics. The introduction of the obstructions created intermediate light lobbies, which materially assisted in overcoming the problem of visual adaptation on entering the casemates.

The lighting studies carried out at the Bartlett greatly assisted the exhibition designer, the positive outcome of this cooperative design process has proved very successful.

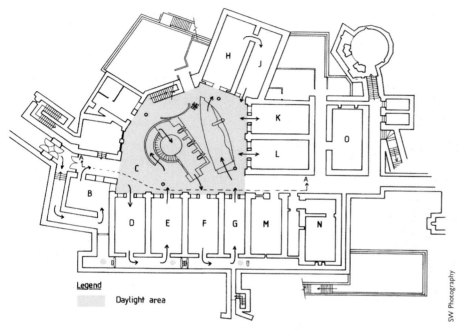

Legend

Daylight area

Plan of the relationship of the central courtyard with the surrounding casemates

The central courtyard

Exterior of the tent structure

Exhibition in the gallery above the courtyard/ daylit

SW Photography

Exhibition inside one of the casemates

SW Photography

TRANSPORT

Jubilee Line Underground

INTRODUCTION

The extension to the Jubilee Line Underground in London, which runs from Westminster eastwards as far as Stratford was completed in 1999, and is a fine example of engineering in the field of transport. In most cases daylight has been introduced to the lower areas of the stations, by various means, such as domes, drums, canopies and light shafts.

Roland Paoletti, the architect in overall charge was, as Frank Pick before him, conscious of the opportunity to create buildings of quality; but rather than imposing some form of grand design on his project architects, he relied first on choosing those architects with particular engineering skills, and then allowing them to work within the framework of the local community to express the grain of an individual neighbourhood.

In selecting four Underground stations to feature in this Case Study of the Jubilee Line, the purpose was not to provide a 'beauty contest,' since the architectural quality of all the new stations along the line is significant, but to choose stations in which the solutions to the problems posed by daylighting stations on the Jubilee Line are noted for their differences of approach.

The examples chosen are as follows:

Southwark
Natural light funnelled down through four storeys by means of a wide concealed cone structure.

Canada Water
A glazed cylindrical ticket hall at ground level allows light to filter gently down to the escalators below, with dynamic patterns of sunlight and shadow.

Canary Wharf
Three wide glazed canopies located above the vertical circulation at the escalator locations, provides ample daylight in the spaces below for orientation and daylight impression.

Stratford
The situation is entirely different. First it is an 'above ground' Underground station, in which the passenger enters the trains which run inside the building at the same level as the ticket office.

The architects for the four selected stations are as follows:

Southwark
McCormac Jamieson Prichard
Canada Water
Ron Herron/Imagination
Canary Wharf
Foster and Partners
Stratford
Wilkinson Eyre

Jubilee Line Extension – Southwark

McCormac Jamieson Prichard

The Underground station at Southwark contains several distinctly different spaces, being complicated by the requirement to incorporate a link with Waterloo East Railtrack station.

Arriving at Southwark Station you are led by daylit escalators to the 'intermediate concourse' which leads you either down to the main Jubilee Line train level, or upwards to Waterloo East. The intermediate concourse is a key element of circulation.

The concourse is daylit from overhead by means of a cone clad in blue glass patterned in triangles, the daylight through the cone being controlled by 'piranese' like deep louvres. This is an enormously impressive space, and a dignified entrance to the 'world of the train'.

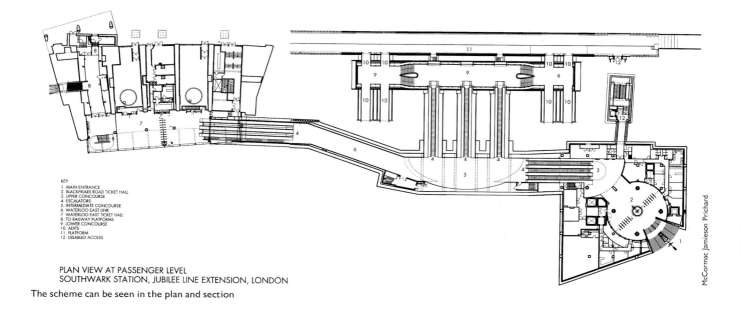

KEY
1. MAIN ENTRANCE
2. BLACKFRIARS ROAD TICKET HALL
3. UPPER CONCOURSE
4. ESCALATORS
5. INTERMEDIATE CONCOURSE
6. WATERLOO EAST LINK
7. WATERLOO EAST TICKET HALL
8. TO RAILWAY PLATFORMS
9. LOWER CONCOURSE
10. ADITS
11. PLATFORM
12. DISABLED ACCESS

McCormac Jamieson Prichard

PLAN VIEW AT PASSENGER LEVEL
SOUTHWARK STATION, JUBILEE LINE EXTENSION, LONDON

The scheme can be seen in the plan and section

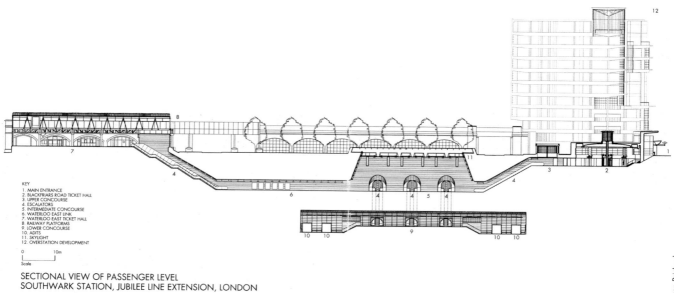

KEY
1. MAIN ENTRANCE
2. BLACKFRIARS ROAD TICKET HALL
3. UPPER CONCOURSE
4. ESCALATORS
5. INTERMEDIATE CONCOURSE
6. WATERLOO EAST LINK
7. WATERLOO EAST TICKET HALL
8. RAILWAY PLATFORMS
9. LOWER CONCOURSE
10. ADITS
11. SKYLIGHT
12. OVERSTATION DEVELOPMENT

0   10m
Scale

SECTIONAL VIEW OF PASSENGER LEVEL
SOUTHWARK STATION, JUBILEE LINE EXTENSION, LONDON

The scheme can be seen in the plan and section

McCormac Jamieson Prichard

The scheme can be seen in the plan and section on p. 178

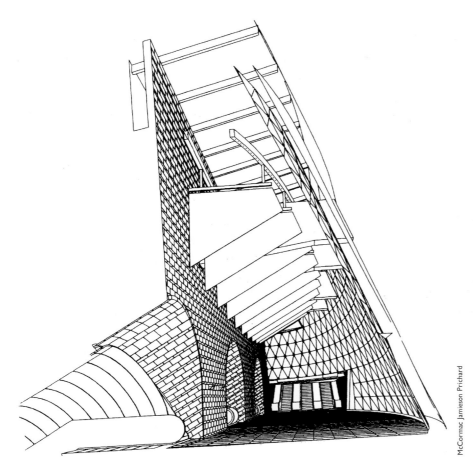

McCormac Jamieson Prichard

The intermediate concourse

DP Archive

Approach from the Jubilee Line escalator

DP Archive

Jubilee Line Extension – Canada Water   Ron Herron/Imagination

Whilst the daylighting at Southwark is not evident above ground, being achieved by the source of daylight concealed in the cone; the daylight at Canada Water makes its presence felt at street level by an entrance in the form of a large glazed entrance cylinder.

The cylinder acts as a daylight lantern to the escalator halls below, and funnels daylight deep into the building, providing a dynamic shadow pattern to the hall.

This is very much in the tradition of some of Chas. Holden's original stations such as

Arnos Grove, but with a much clearer daylight orientation.

Ron Herron/Imagination

Axonometric of the station to illustrate the form of daylighting

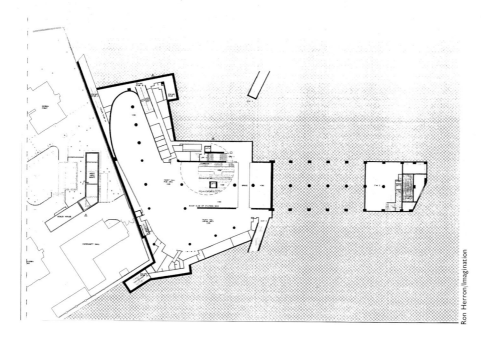

Ron Herron/Imagination

Plan at ground level

The glazed entrance hall, Canada Water

Daylight from the entrance cylinder

Daylight patterns in the escalator hall at lower level

Jubilee Line Extension – Canary Wharf

Foster and Partners

Canary Wharf is the largest of the Jubilee Line Underground stations, and is designed to cater for the population of the Canary Wharf business community, which, when complete, will number at peak periods more than those using the Underground at Oxford Circus.

The station is built within the space originally occupied by the West India dock. The complex is 313 m long by 35 m wide but little of this shows above ground, which is landscaped as parkland, apart from three glazed canopies covering the entrances.

It is these glazed canopies which direct daylight deep into the station concourse, providing the particular quality of light to the interior; this needs to be experienced personally, although the accompanying photographs are helpful in establishing an impression of the visual environment below ground.

Outside at night the canopies glow with light giving orientation to the parkland which acts as the main public recreation space for the Canary Wharf community, whilst during the day the trees and water gardens create a sense of peace and tranquillity.

Long section

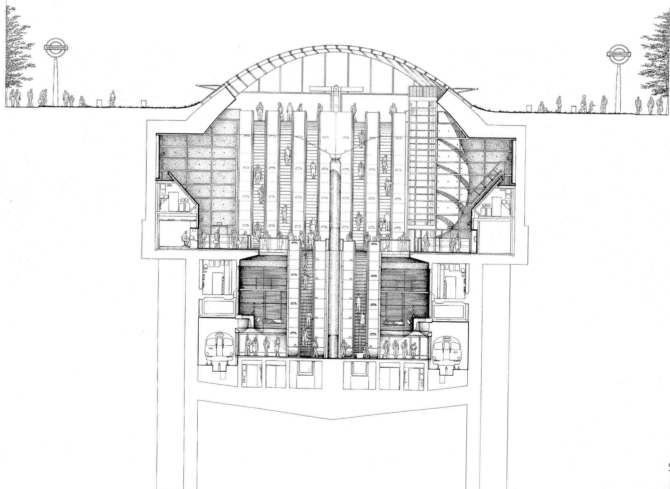

Cross section

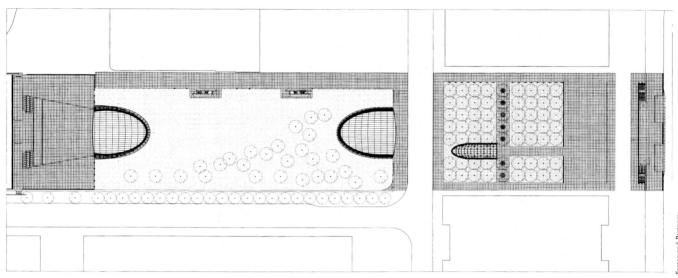

Site/roof plan

Foster and Partners

Entrance canopy

DP Archive

View up escalators to daylit canopy

DP Archive

Parkland at site level

DP Archive

The ticket hall

Dennis Gilbert/View

Ticket hall, long view

Nigel/Young, Foster and Partners

Jubilee Line Extension – Stratford   Wilkinson Eyre

The situation here is entirely different. It is an 'above ground' station, in which passengers enter the trains which run inside the building at the same level as the ticket office.

There are two storeys, required to allow passengers to walk above the trains along the rear of the hall.

The daylighting problem was solved more by the nature of the structure, since this in itself ensured a building of sufficient height,

more akin to a sports hall, with its large areas of high level glazing around all sides of the building. The final solution, with its solid roof and large side windows, provides a well daylit space where, during the day, there is no need for artificial lighting any more than there would be on an open platform.

The curved soffit to the underside of the roof was designed in collaboration with the UCL Laboratories as a reflecting light surface

to bounce light down into the concourse space. This has been achieved by the design of a purpose made aluminium extrusion, perforated for acoustic purposes.

To ensure that the ceiling does not appear dark in contrast, it is uplit by artificial lighting from specially designed uplighters mounted on the maintenance gantry at low level. These throw light up to the ceiling and provide an even intensity of light in the concourse.

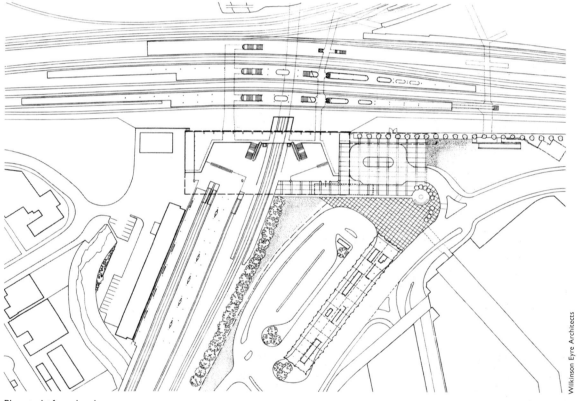

Plan at platform level

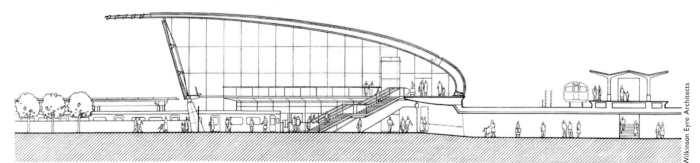

Section

Exterior view to entrance

General view down length of concourse

View of concourse from first floor
level

INDUSTRIAL

Cummins Power Generation

Architect	Bennetts Associates
Engineer	Ernest Griffiths and Sons
Client	Cummins Engine Company

As a client the Cummins Engine Co. of America is an active promoter of sound architecture; their corporate HQ in the US being noted for a catalogue of thoroughbred public and institutional buildings, whilst in this country the tradition has been carried on, of which the Cummins Power Generation plant by Bennetts Associates is no exception.

In the US there has been a tradition of windowless factories (as sadly also of windowless schools) leading to high levels of concern as to the psychological effect on the workforce, though Cummins have led a change in attitude away from this approach in recent work.

In the UK there is now an ethos of work spaces providing adequate levels of daylighting and the method of daylighting adopted at Cummins is a further example of this.

The central lines of rooflights which follow the lines of the three bays of the building, together with the clerestory windows along

the sides, flood the building with natural light, even allowing a welcome degree of sunlight to enter.

The brief to the architects was for a general light level of 500 lux, and this can be maintained by the pattern of metal halide high bay light fittings at all times, but during the day when there is ample daylight outside the building, some rows of the artificial lights may be switched off, when the level of daylight approaches 700 lux or more in the interior.

There is no sophisticated daylight linking control, and the payback for such controls in terms of energy saving should be considered. This would have to address the problem that the metal halide lamp is not amenable to dimming.

The exterior elevations of the building do not suggest the building's daylight credibility, since the rooflighting is not immediately apparent; but it can be seen that the daylighting available from the low level

windows along the south-western face provide a welcome degree of high contrast in an area used for circulation rather than production. Another important factor is that the specialist floor specified provides a light reflective finish, unusual in a factory making heavy metal generator equipment.

As is the case with most modern offices, the use of computer screens ensures that the side windows which apparently cause unacceptable glare tend to be monitored by venetian blinds. As computer screens are developed and 'flattened' this may prove to be unnecessary.

One effect of being close to the flight path of Manston Airport, is that after two years the outer surface of the rooflights suffer from a thin layer of aviation film, which diminishes the level of daylight to the interior, an aspect which requires determined maintenance if the level of the daylight is to be maintained.

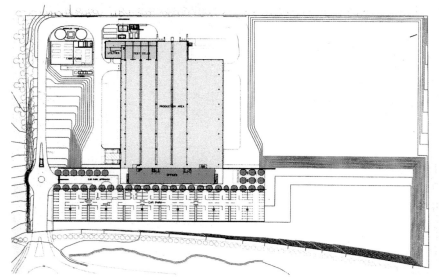

Bennetts Associates

The plan of the complex

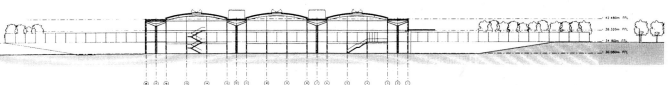

Bennetts Associates

Cross section through the three bays

Long section, showing the relationship with the offices, at one end

Bennetts Associates

Daylight entering through low level windows to the western elevation

DP Archive

General view of the interior of the factory

DP Archive

View up to the lines of rooflights

DP Archive

The south-eastern elevation

DP Archive

Gridshell Building, Weald and Downland Museum

Architect   Edward Cullinan Architects

Engineer   Buro Happold

Client   Weald and Downland Open Air Museum, Singleton. Sponsors: Heritage Lottery Fund. Jerwood Foundation.

The Gridshell is essentially an industrial building, a no-frills solution to the problem posed by the museum, for a large tall open space where the timbers and frames of historic buildings can be laid out for conservation and repair, before being erected on the site of the museum. It is further used for training courses in conservation.

The design objectives for the project were for sustainable construction and energy efficiency; an early decision was made that daylighting should provide the principal means of illumination. Artificial light was seen as a necessary supplementary provision for extended hours usage, or in extreme winter conditions.

The primary use for the building required a large tall open space free of obstruction for the conservation work, with a smaller area for use as a museum and storing of the museum's artefacts. Whilst the former required a high level of energy efficient lighting, which was interpreted as daylighting during the day, the artefacts store would have intermittent use and might therefore be met by artificial light at all times.

The architect Edward Cullinan's sketch design illustrates the concept for the building, showing the tall 'conservation space' above ground level, well daylit from roof lighting, whilst the 'artefacts store' is placed at a lower level cut into the chalk hillside, artificially lit when in use.

The lightweight Gridshell structure designed by Buro Happold has been well documented elsewhere, but the purpose of this Case Study is to illustrate the nature and quality of the daylighting, together with its implication in terms of energy, for this is a 'green' building in which 'sustainability' and energy efficiency is all a part of the ethos of the museum itself.

Three important considerations were apparent:

1. The roof should contain a high degree of transparency.
2. The internal finishes should be light in colour to improve contrast rendering.
3. A balance was to be found between the need for a high level of daylight, and the need to control solar gain.

The daylighting consists of continuous rows of polycarbonate sheeting at high level, which on the north side is 'clear', letting in maximum daylight, and on the south side it has a 'bronze tint' to reduce possible sun glare. Looking up from inside the building the effect of this change is visible but not disturbing, and the impression at floor level is of an even light, ideal for the needs of conservation work. The consistency of the northern light, complemented by the variability of the southern light, formed the final scheme proposal, the rooflights being installed along the full length of the roof, to

ensure acceptable contrast, the result being an even quality of daylighting, suitable for all seasonable conditions.

The use of polycarbonate sheeting in place of glass, whilst having an impact on reducing the cost, was primarily because of its light weight for erection purposes. There is a large area of glazing and if any form of glass had been specified its weight would have been a factor.

For work after dark a sufficient level of artificial light is available from a pattern of downlights, visible in the photographs.

The building was completed in May 2002 and so far there has been no need for artificial lighting to be used during the day, although both conservation work and course tuition have been in progress. The fact that no electricity has been used for lighting the space during the day is evidence of the building's energy efficiency, a strategy carried through for the building's heating and cooling.

By sinking the building into the slope of the hillside it reduced the environmental impact of the building on its surroundings, and whilst it is a large building, one is not conscious of this when visiting the site.

To sum up, the strategy for the building has been proved to be successful; so much so that the building won an RIBA architecture award, and was shortlisted for the Stirling Prize.

The final result is an enclosed space with a high level of daylight provision, estimated to provide a Daylight Factor (DF) of 10 per cent.

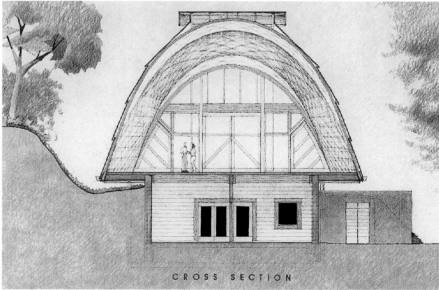

CROSS SECTION

Edward Cullinan

Sketch section of the new building

View of the exterior timber walling and high level daylight sheeting

Interior of main conservation space

View towards the west end, emphasizing the view out

Bibliography

Baker Fanchiotti and Steemers, *Daylighting in Architecture*, A European Reference Book, James and James, 1993

Baker, Nick and Koen, Steemers, *Daylight Design of Buildings*, James and James, 2002

Boyce, P.R., *Human Factors in Lighting*, Applied Science Publishers, London, 1981

BRE, 1985, *Lighting Controls and Daylight Use*

Button, D. and Pye, B., *Glass in Buildings, A Guide to Modern Architecture Glass Performance*, Butterworth Architecture, 1993

Cuttle, Christopher, *Lighting by Design*, Architectural Press, Oxford, 2003

DETR, *Desktop Guide to Daylighting*, Good Practice Guide, 245

Evans, B.H., *Daylight in Architecture*, McGraw-Hill, NY, 1981

Fuller Moore, *Concepts and Practice of Architectural Daylighting*, Van Nostrand Reinhold, 1985

Gardner, C. and Hannaford, B., *Lighting Design. An introductory guide*, Design Council, London, 1993

Hopkinson, R.G., Petherbridge, P. and Longmore, J., *Daylighting*, Heinemann, London, 1966

Hopkinson and Kay, *The Lighting of Buildings*, Faber & Faber, 1972

Kahn, Louis and the Kimbell Museum, Neil E. Johnson, Kimbell Art Foundation, *Light is the Theme*, Fort Worth, Texas, 1975

Lam, William C. *Sunlighting as Formgiver for Architecture*, Van Nostrand Reinhold, NY, 1986

Littlefair, P.J., *Daylight Sunlight and Lighting Control*, BRE, 1980

Littlefair, P.J., *Average Daylight Factor. A simple basis for daylight design*, BRE, 1988

Loe, David and Mansfield, K., *Daylighting Design in Architecture*, BRECSU/ BRE, 1998

Loe, David and Mansfield, K.P. *Daylighting Design in Architecture*, BRECSU, Building Research Establishment, 1998

Loe, David and Rowlands, E., *The Art and Science of Lighting: A Strategy for Lighting Design*, LR & T/CIBSE 28 No. 4. 1996

Lloyd Jones, David, *Architecture and the Environment*, Laurence King, 1998

Olgyay, Aladar and Olgyay, Victor, *Solar Control and Shading Devices*, 1957

Phillips, Derek, *Lighting Modern Buildings*, Architectural Press, 2000

Slater, A.I., *Lighting Controls, An essential element of Energy Efficient Lighting*, BRE, 1987

Steen Eiler Rasmussen, *Experiencing Architecture*, MIT Press, 1992

Tregenza, Peter and Loe, David, *The Design of Lighting*, E. & F.N. Spon, 1998

CIBSE PUBLICATIONS

Code for Interior Lighting, London, 1994
The Outdoor Environment, LG6, 1992
Designing Buildings for Daylight, James Bell and William Burt, 1995
Daylighting and Window Design, Lighting Guide LG. 10, 1999
Daylighting in Buildings, University College Dublin, for European Commission, 1994

PAPERS

Bell, J.A.M., Burt, W., *Designing Buildings for Daylight*, Building Research Establishment, Watford, 1995.

Building Research Establishment (BRE), *Energy Conservation in Artificial Lighting*, BRE, Watford, UK, 1979.

Building Research Establishment (BRE), *Office Lighting for Good Visual Task Conditions*, BRE, Watford, UK, 1981.

Building Research Establishment (BRE), *Lighting Controls and Daylight Use*, BRE, Watford, UK, 1985.

Chartered Institution of Building Services Engineers. *Code for Interior Lighting*, CIBSE, London, 1994.

Littlefair, P.J. *Innovative Daylighting*. Review of systems and evaluation methods. BRE Lighting Research and Technology, 1990

Littlefair, P.J., *Designing with Innovative Daylighting Systems*, Building Research Establishment, Watford, UK, 1996.

Phillips, Derek, *Space, Time and Architecture*, Presidential address to the Illuminating Engineering Society, 1974

Phillips, Derek, *Architecture Day and Night*, CIBSE National Lighting Conference, 1992

Phillips, Derek, *Daylighting in Architecture*, Birmingham NEC, RIBA/CPD West Midlands Region, 1993

Phillips, Derek, *Lighting and Interior Architecture*, Lux Europa, 1993

Rasmussen, S.E., *Experiencing Architecture*, The M.I.T. Press, Cambridge, Mass., 1964.

CONFERENCES

New Light on Windows, RIBA, November 1996
Daylighting Design and Research, CIBSE Daylight Group/RIBA, October 2000

Glossary

A simplified explanation of references used in the text divided into the following eight headings. Use the Index for page references. This is similar to the Glossary used in *The Lit Environment*,[1] which will enable the two books to be used together.

1. SEEING/PERCEPTION
2. LIGHT SOURCES/DAYLIGHT
3. LIGHT SOURCES/OTHER THAN DAYLIGHT (artificial)
4. LIGHTING TERMINOLOGY
5. LIGHTING METHODS
6. ENERGY AND CONTROLS
7. ARCHITECTURE
8. GLAZING TYPES/DAYLIGHT CONTROLS

I. SEEING/PERCEPTION

Adaptation   The human eye can adapt to widely differeing levels of light, but not at the same time. When entering a darkened space from a brightly lit space, the eye needs time to adapt, to the general lighting conditions; this is known as 'adaptation'.

Clarity   Clearness, unambiguous.

Contrast   The visual difference between the colour or brightness of two surfaces when seen together. Too high a contrast can be the cause of glare.

Modelling   The modelling of an object derives from the direction and intensity of the light falling upon its surfaces, which provides the shadow patterns leading to an understanding of its form.

Perception   Receiving impressions of one's environment primarily by means of vision, but also one's other senses; providing a totality of experience.

Quality, a degree of excellence   The 'quality' of a lighting design derives from a series of different elements, the most important of which is 'unity',

---

[1] Phillips, D. (2002) *Lighting Modern buildings*, Architectural Press.

but which also includes aspects such as modelling, variety, colour and clarity.

Unity   The quality or impression of being a single entity or whole; this can be applied equally to a small or large complex, the word 'holism' is often used in its place.

Variety   The quality of change over time in brightness, contrast and appearance of a space, or series of spaces.

Virtual image   An image of a subject or lit space formed in a computer, which can be used to provide a visual impression of the lighting design in order to explain a proposal.

Visual acuity   A measure of the eye's ability to discern detail.

Visual task/task light   The visual element of doing a job of work, and any local or concentrated light fitting placed to improve visibility.

2. LIGHT SOURCES/DAYLIGHT

Artificial sky   A research tool in the form of a "light box" where levels of light may be measured in architectural models placed within. Sophisticated artificial skies exist whereby the light can be varied to replicate the exterior light and sun paths at different seasons and climates. The opportunity exists for miniature photography of interiors, and visual inspection of the interior by the architect.

Average daylight factor   An analysis of the Daylight Factors in an interior to gain an overall or average view of the daylighting in a space.

Bilateral daylight   Daylight from both sides of a building.

Daylight   The light received from the sun and the sky, which varies throughout the day, as modified by the seasons and the weather.

Daylight effective depth   The distance from a window which allows daylight to penetrate to achieve a desired Daylight Factor.

Daylight factor (DF)   The ratio of the light received at a point within a building, expressed as a percentage of that available externally. Since daylight varies continually the amount of light from a given DF is not a finite figure, but gives a good indication of the level of daylight available.

Daylight linking   Controls which vary the level of artificial light inside a building, relating this to the available daylight.

Electrochromic glass   Glass designed to respond indirectly to an electric current which alters its transmission value

Georgian window   The standard sash window for domestic use in the eighteenth century in England, combining clear daylight, with view and ventilation.

Heliostats   A system of mirrors placed at roof level which can be energised to track the sun, and redirect it into a building.

Indirect daylighting   Similar to indirect artificial lighting, whereby the light from "windows" is concealed from the view of the building occupants giving light to surfaces and objects within a space. This has particular relevance in churches.

Innovative daylighting   Methods of daylight admission to a building which take advantage of a new technology: examples being Light Shelves, Light Pipes, or heliostates etc.

Interactive window   A prototype window design, combining the requirements of daylighting and view, with those of solar control, and ventilation, thermal and sound insulation and the elimination of glare.

Light penetration   See daylight effective depth.

Light pipes   A form of rooflight associates with mirror finished ducts which direct natural light and sometimes ventilation into lower floors of the building.

Light shelves   A horizontal construction at the window designed to reflect light to the ceiling, to assist in increasing the daylight penetration into the room

Low emissivity glass   Glass where the radiating power of heat or light is reduced

No sky-line   The demarkation line within a building where, due to external obstruction and window configuration, no view of the sky is visible.

Obstruction/view   The diminution of available light and view by other buildings at a distance. View is an important environmental aspect of daylight, which may be impaired by obstruction, but can sometimes be overcome by attention to orientation.

Orientation   The geographical relationship of a proposed building to its site, enabling a strategic view to be gained of the possible daylighting design.

Physical modelling   The use of architectural models to provide a means of calculating the daylight factors of a proposed building design. These can be placed in an artificial sky or used externally. Physical modelling has been found to mimic methods of computer calculation sufficiently accurately with the added advantage of providing a visual impression of the interior to the architect.

Photochromic glass   Glass responding directly, to an environment stimulus such as heat or light, which alters its transmission value

Prismatic panels   Panels formed to alter the path of light, so as to redirect it, either to cut out glare, or to introduce light for useful purposes

Rights of light   Legislation which allows a building owner to preserve the amount of natural light his building enjoys; likewise he must ensure that his building does not obstruct the daylight enjoyed by his neighbour.

Shading/briese soleil   The means adopted to prevent the deleterious effects of solar gain from southern exposures; these may be external structural louvres attached to the face of the building or forms of helioscreen blind.

Sky glare   The unacceptable contrast between the view of the sky outside, and the interior surfaces.

Skylight   The light received from the whole vault of the sky as modified by the weather and time of day, ignoring sunlight.

Solar gain   Heat derived from the sun; whilst generally therapeutic, it may require control by forms of blind, louvre or solar glass.

Solar glass   Glass designed to reflect a percentage of direct heat (infra red) from the sun.

Solar panels   Panels applied mostly to south facing façades of buildings designed to generate electricity from the sun. This can be used for heating water or for lighting.

Solar shading   The mechanical means by louvre, blind or special glazing, to eliminate glare from the sun. External means are the most efficient, but can suffer from long term maintenance.

Sunlight   The light received directly from the sun, as opposed to that derived from the sky.

Sunpath   The sun's orbit. As the earth travels around the sun, variations occur both throughout the day and the seasons; these changes in position are known as the 'Sunpath'. This can be accurately predicted.

Sustainability   Applied to development which meets the needs of the present, and is at least as valuable to future generations, as the value of the environmental exploitation that results. This can be applied to the concept of nett zero energy demand.

View   The scene beyond a window which can be enjoyed from within a space. The importance of this should not be underestimated.

Window   'Wind-eyes' take many forms, to provide daylight to an interior.

3.   LIGHT SOURCES OTHER THAN DAYLIGHT/ ARTIFICIAL

Arc light   The first form of electric light derived by passing an electric current between two electrodes. Developed by Sir Humphery Davy in 1809.

Candles   Candles are made by moulding wax or other flammable material around a wick, which sustains a flame to give light. Modern candles are clean, do not 'gutter', and provide light of a particular quality suitable for social occasions. There have been many light sources which attempt to imitate the quality of 'candle light'; most fail completely, while one or two later versions achieve some success.

Electric light   The development by Edison and Swan of the 'incandescent' lamp in the nineteenth century and the arc lamp, providing the foundation of all modern forms of light derived from electricity.

Electric light sources   These lamps are described in detail in Chapter 5, and are listed here.

Incandescent sources
tungsten filament
tungsten halogen
low voltage tungsten halogen

Discharge sources
cold cathode (fluorescent)
mercury fluorescent (high and low pressure)
low pressure sodium
high pressure sodium
high pressure mercury
metal halide (inc. ceramic arc)

Fluorescent lamps
halophosphor – tubular fluorescent triphosphor
compact fluorescent
induction lamps

Fibre optics (remote source)   At its simplest, it is the transfer from a light source placed in one position to light emitted in another, by means of glass fibre or polymer strands.

Fluorescent phosphors   The internal coatings on surfaces of mercury discharge lamps which produce 'visible' light when excited by the ultra-violet rays emitted by the discharge. The phosphors determine the colour of the visible light.

Gaslight   The light derived from burning coal gas, developed in the late eighteenth century, and widely used during the nineteenth century both for domestic and industrial use.

Oil lamps   These together with firelight are the earliest forms of artificial light source, the oil being derived from animals, birds or fish. Hollowed out stone dishes and later clay pots were used with some form of wick. Oil lamps survived until the nineteenth century with the development of the 'Argand' lamp.

4. LIGHTING TERMINOLOGY

Angle of separation   The angle between the line of sight and the light fitting. The smaller this is, the more likely the light will be glaring.

Brightness   The subjective appearance of a lit surface; dependent upon the luminance of the surface and a person's adaptation.

Bulk lamp replacement   The replacement 'en masse' of the lamps in a lighting system when it is calculated that a percentage of the lamps will fail, and that the light output of the system will fall below the design level.

Colour   We accept that we only see true colour under daylight, despite the fact that this varies considerably throughout the day. All artificial sources distort colour in one way or another.

Colour renderng   A comparison between the colour appearance of a surface under natural light and that from an artificial source.

Efficiency/efficacy   The ratio of the light output from the lamp, toe nergy consumed in lumens/watt.

Flicker   The rapid variation in light from discharge sources due to the 50 Hz mains supply, which can cause unpleasant sensations. With the development of high frequency gear the problem is overcome.

Glare/reflected glare   The most important 'negative' aspect of quality. There are two types of glare, 'discomfort and disability.' Both types are the result of too great a contrast. Glare may result from both daylighting or artificial lighting, either directly or by reflection and must be avoided at the design stage.

Illumination level   The amount of light falling on a surface expressed in engineering terms as lumens per square metre (or Lux) and known as 'illuminance'.

Intensity   Refers to the power of a light source to emit light in a given direction.

Light fitting/luminaire   The housing for the light source which is used to distribute the light. While the technical word is 'luminaire,' the more descriptive 'light fitting' is still widely used. The 'housing' provides the support, electrical connection and suitable optical control.

Luminance   Light emitted or reflected from a surface in a particular direction; the result of the illumination level and the reflectance.

Lux   The measure of 'illumination level' (illuminance) in lumen/sq.m. The Foot Candle is used in the USA, meaning 1 lumen per square foot or 10.76 Lux.

Maintenance factor   The factor applied to the initial illumination level, to take account of dirst accumulation and fall off in light output from the lamp, when calculating the level of useful light.

Reflectance   The ratio of light reflected from a surface to the light falling upon it; as affected by the lightness or darkness of the surface.

Reflection factor   The ratio of the light reflected from a surface, to the light falling upon it. The surface, whether shiny or matt, will affect the nature of the reflected light.

Scalloping   The effect gained from placing a row of light fittings too close to a wall. Where intended this effect can be pleasing, but more generally it becomes an unwanted intrusion on the space.

Sparkle   A word which may be applied to rapid changes to light over time, most readily applied to the flicker of candlelight or firelight; sparkle may be applied to reflected or refracted light from small facets, such as those of a glass chandelier.

5   LIGHTING METHODS

Ceiling/wall mounted   The method by which light fittings are supported directly from the ceiling or wall.

Concealed lighting   Concealed in the ceiling or wall configuration, to provide light on to adjacent surfaces.

Decorative lighting   That which is designed to be seen and enjoyed for its own sake, such as a crystal chandelier. Alternatively it may be light directed on to objects to achieve a decorative purpose.

Downlight   Light fittings giving their main light downwards; these are generally recessed and include both wide beam and narrow angles.

Emergency lighting   The lighting system designed to operate in the event of power failure to facilitate the evacuation of a building, or continuation of essential services. Various methods adopted to ensure a suitable source of power.

Floodlighting   Generally refers to the exterior lighting of a building at night, by means of lights with controlled beams placed at a distance.

Functional lighting   Lighting which is planned to provide light to satisfy the practical needs of a space.

General   Diffusing light fittings giving all round light.

Indirect   Lighting provided 'indirectly' reflected from ceiling or wall.

Local light/task light   A light fitting designed to light a specific task, generally at individual control.

Louvres/baffles   A means of shielding the light from a fitting or from daylight, to eliminate glare. They can be fixed or moveable.

Portable light fittings   Such as table and floor standards designed to provide local light. 'Portable' uplights a useful addition.

Raising and lowering gear   The apparatus applied to heavy 'light fittings' in tall spaces, to allow them to be lowered for lamp change and maintenance.

Spotlight   Light fittings designed to throw light in beams of varying width and intensity.

Suspended   The pendant method of 'hanging' a light fitting from the ceiling or roof.

Torchere   Originally a decorative free standing 'candle holder'; a term sometimes applied to modern wall brackets.

Track mounted light fittings   Both supported and energized, from the numerous track systems available; giving flexibility.

Uplight   Light fittings directing their light up to the ceiling providing indirect light.

Wall washing   The means of lighting by which a wall is designed to be lit evenly; several methods can be adopted to achieve this, some more successful than others.

6.   ENERGY AND CONTROLS

BEMS   Building Energy Management Systems. A means of computer control of lighting systems within a building.

Biomass   A source of renewable energy which can be used in a building for activating building services, such as "rape seed oil".

Control gear   Discharge sources require 'control gear' comprising amongst others: starters igniters transformers, capacitors, ballasts and chokes to operate. Incandescent lamps require no gear, giving low initial cost and making dimming simple.

Digital multiplex controller   A sophisticated electronic controller used to monitor and vary circuits in a lighting system, such as might be used in a theatre.

Dimming   Dimming controls are exactly what the name implies, a device by which the intensity of a light source can be reduced. All filament sources, both mains and low voltage can be controlled by simple dimmers.

Intelligent luminaires   Light fittings with inbuilt sensors programmed to vary the light intensity, generally related to the amount of available daylight or occupancy.

Noise attenuation   Noise reduction.

Passive building   A building which by its configuration eliminates the need for mechanical ventilation, and reduces the need for daytime electric lighting

Photocell   Measures illuminance at any position. When placed externally the photocell allows internal light control systems to react to changes in the weather, an element of 'daylight linking'.

Photovoltaics   External panels on the southern exposure of a building designed to convert solar energy into useful electricity, a developing technology.

Scene set   The use of more complicated electronic controls using a microprocessor, to permit different room appearances to be available at the touch of a button, with a number of scenes being 'present'; which can subsequently be changed automatically.

Stack effect   The way in which hot air will rise in a chimney.

Thermal shutter   An electrically operated mirror which tracks the sun, and redirects its rays to cope with low or high angle sun, at different seasons of the year.

Wind turbine   A 'windmill' designed to generate electricity.

7. ARCHITECTURE

Atrium   The courtyard entrance to a roman house, with an opening in the centre through which rainwater was collected. This opening also provided light to the courtyard and surrounding rooms. The word has now taken on the meaning of multistorey spaces which are daylit from overhead glazed roofs.

Barrel vault   A continuous structural vault of semi-circular section, used from Roman architecture to the present; nowadays formed of reinforced concrete.

Brieze soleil   Large vertical louvres externally designed to control the heat and glare from the sun. These are most used in hot climates.

Casemate   A vaulted chamber built into a fortress for defence. Often used as a battery, or barracks.

Ceiling coffer A form of concrete roof construction, where, to add strength without increased weight, square holes or 'coffers' are omitted leaving a 'waffle' shape into which services can be placed.

Clerestorey (also clear-storey, and pronounced this way) The upper storey with windows above the side aisle roofs, giving high level daylight particularly in a church.

Conservation The protection of works of art against the deleterous effects of the environment. The control of light levels (particularly ultra violet) is a major component of conservation.

Dimensional cooardination The manner in which different building materials are planned to fit together.

Floor plate A modern term meaning the plan of a building at each of its levels.

Flying buttress An external abutment designed to take the horizontal thrust from an internal arch in a building. This was a device used in the mediaeval cathedral to permit lightweight construction of the external wall, akin to the curtain walls of today.

Folded plate Ceiling development of shell concrete construction.

Glass brick The development of 'bricks' made from glass in the 1930s allowed architects to design structural 'see-through' walls. The Maison Verre in Paris is a well-known modern example; although not widely used today they remain a useful architects tool.

Lighting gantry A light weight 'bridge' independent of the main structure of a building, providing support and electric power to light fittings.

Roof monitors/laylights The roof construction in which daylight is permitted to enter a space from overhead. In the case of factories they would be designed to control the entry of sunlight.

Roof truss A development of the beam supports to a roof allowing an openwork lattice to accept services.

Scale Scale is a matter of 'proportion,' the larger the scale, the less human the building will appear. It is sometimes difficult to judge the size of a particular building or interior until a person is added to give it 'scale'.

Shell concrete A thin skin of reinforced concrete, formed in a curve to span the roofs of large areas.

Spandrel The infill defining the floor level in modern building.

Sprinkler system Fire control by means of a system of water pipes which are designed to deluge water to douse a fire, when design temperatures are exceeded.

Sustainable building Applied to development which meets the needs of the present, and is at least as valuable to future generations, as the value of the environment exploitation that results. This can be applied to the concept of "net zero energy demand".

Undercroft A term in mediaeval architecture depicting the lower level vaulting of a cathedral, above which the main edifice is built.

8. GLAZING TYPES/DAYLIGHT CONTROLS

Clear glass   In terms of window glass this can be of several types and combinations, such as double or triple glazing, its principle characteristic being that it allows the view to the exterior to be unmodified.

Electrochromic glass   Glass designed to respond indirectly to an electric current, which alters its transmission value.

Glass blocks   Glass blocks have seen a recent revival, in allowing a wall which both lets in light and acts as a structural member.

Laminated glass   Glass with internal sheets of plastic, laminated together to provide a sandwich for greater strength. The nature of the sandwich can be designed for different uses, such as U/V protection.

Low emissivity glass   Glass where the radiating power of heat or light is reduced by having a heat reflecting coat applied to it.

Patterned glass   Glasses rolled to give a wide variety of patterns which diffuse the light.

Photochromic glass   Glass responding directly to an environment stimulus, such as heat or light, which alters its transmission value.

Prismatic panels   Panels formed to alter the path of daylight, so as to redirect it either to cut out glare, or to introduce light for useful purposes.

Tinted glass   Applied to glass which is modified by the addition of different materials to achieve a variety of colours such as green, grey, bronze or blue; the thicker the glass the more dense the colour. The glasses provide different light and solar radiant heat transmission characteristics.

Venetian blinds   A time-honoured blind formed of controllable horizontal slats which can be used separately or combined in between sheets of glass to monitor daylight and glare.

Wired glass   Glass with a wire mesh embedded, useful for security.

Index of architects and designers

Architects

Aedas Architects (Originally Abbey Hanson and Rowe), 55
Ahrends Burton and Koralek (ABK), 118
Alec French Partnership, 124, 126
Allies and Morrison, 132
AN Tombazis and Associates, 170
Architects Co-Partnership (ACP), 114
Architects Design Partnership (ADP), 138
Arup Associates, 90
ASL Dangerfield, 172
Avanti Architects, 108
Barnstone and Aubry, 144
Basil Spence, 4
Bennetts Associates, 190
Casson Conder Partnership, 122
Chetwood Associates, 164
Edward Cullinan, 192
Fielden Clegg Bradley, 148
Fletcher Priest, 150
Foster and Partners, 72, 182
Jeremy Johnson-Marshall, 98
Jestico + Whiles, 136
Jim Mc. Reynolds Partners. (USA)

John McAslan and Partners, 128
Le Corbusier, 29
Manser Associates, 102
McCormac Jamieson Prichard, 178
Michael Hopkins and Partners, 82
Office of Public Works, Dublin, 168
Percy Thomas Partnership, 94
Philip Johnson, 144
R. Smitt, Royal Academy, 162
Richard Rogers Partnership, 78
Ron Herron/Imagination, 180
Squire and Partners, 86
Studio E Architects, 156
Toyo Ito, 154
Venturi Scott Brown and Associates, 76
Wilkinson Eyre, 186
William Wenzler and Associates (USA), 142

Lighting designers

Arup Lighting, 94, 128, 144, 154
Bartenbach Lictabor, 170
Brian Ford Associates, 148

Building Research Establishment, 138
Cabinet Berthon, 76
Claude Engle, 72
DPA Lighting Consultants, 102, 162, 172
Halcrow, 136
Justin de Syllas, 108
London Metropolitan University, 170
Pinniger and Partners, 164
Slender Winter Partnership, 138
Squire and Partners, 86
William Lam Associates, 142

Engineers

Buro Happold, 122, 192
Ernest Griffiths and Son, 190
Hoare Lea, 94
Max Fordham, 132
Ove Arup and Partners, 78, 82, 118
Sutton Vane Associates, 168
TG Armstrong and Partners, 114
TME Engineers, 150
Wicheloe MacFarlane, BDP, 124

Subject Index

Architectural Press

An imprint of Elsevier
www.architecturalpress.com

Visit www.architecturalpress.com

Our regularly updated website includes:

- News on our latest books
- Special offers, discounts and freebies
- Free downloadable sample chapters from our newest titles
- Links to companion websites giving you extra information on our books
- Author biographies and information
- Links to useful websites and extensive directories of relevant organisations and publications
- A search engine and a secure online ordering system for the entire catalogue of **Architectural Press** books

You can also get **free membership** of our **eNews** service by visiting our website to register. Once you are a member, you will receive a monthly email bulletin which gives you:

- Exclusive author articles
- The chance to enter prize draws for free books
- Access to offers and discounts exclusive to **eNews** members
- News of our latest books sent direct to your desktop

If you would like any other information about **www.architecturalpress.com** or our **eNews** service please contact:

Rachel Lace, Product Manager
Email: r.lace@elsevier.com
Tel: +44 (0) 1865 314594
Fax: +44 (0)1865 314572
Address: Architectural Press, Linacre House, Jordan Hill, Oxford, OX2 8DP, UK